Angular Design Patterns and Best Practices

Create scalable and adaptable applications that grow to meet
evolving user needs

Alvaro Camillo Neto

Angular Design Patterns and Best Practices

Group Product Manager: Rohit Rajkumar
Publishing Product Manager: Kushal Dave
Book Project Manager: Shagun Saini
Senior Editor: Rakhi Patel
Technical Editor: K Bimala Singha
Copy Editor: Safis Editing
Proofreader: Safis Editing
Indexer: Tejal Daruwale Soni
Production Designer: Ponraj Dhandapani
DevRel Marketing Coordinators: Namita Velgekar and Nivedita Pandey

First published: February 2024

Production reference: 2120124

Published by Packt Publishing Ltd.
Grosvenor House
11 St Paul's Square
Birmingham
B3 1RB, UK

ISBN 978-1-83763-197-1

www.packtpub.com

To my wife, Luciana Gonçalo Balardini Camillo, for being my wonderful beloved partner who did the most important work of taking care of our beloved children, Mario and Gabriel, while I worked on the book. I love you so much my Linda.

– Alvaro Camillo Neto

Foreword

In the ever-evolving landscape of the web, Angular continues to emerge as a beacon of innovation and efficiency, in a continual era of renaissance, and I am thrilled to introduce you to a comprehensive guide authored by a true enthusiast and expert, Alvaro.

This book is a testament to Alvaro's tireless efforts to share his knowledge in the most exciting and up-to-date manner possible. Whether you are a seasoned developer seeking to sharpen your skills or a newcomer eager to dive into the world of Angular, this guide promises to be your trusted companion.

So, embark on this adventure with this book as your guide. May the knowledge within these pages inspire you and empower your journey into the universe of web development, with batteries included for this awesome JavaScript framework, which will always have a module and patterns for what you need.

Happy coding!

William Grasel (`https://www.linkedin.com/in/willgm/?originalSubdomain=br`)

Principal Software Engineer, Stone Inc

With great excitement and admiration, I write this foreword for my dear friend Alvaro's book, *Angular Design Patterns and Best Practices*. For anyone familiar with the Angular framework and seeking to elevate their skills and projects, this book is an invaluable resource.

Alvaro, a Google Developer Expert in Angular and a friend, has poured his wealth of knowledge and practical experience into this comprehensive guide. In *Part 1, Reinforcing the Foundations*, he skilfully navigates essential topics, starting by reinforcing the foundations of Angular development by delving into project setup, application organization, TypeScript patterns, and service implementation, including the Singleton pattern.

Then, *Part 2, Leveraging Angular's Capabili*ties equips you with advanced techniques to handle user input through forms, enhance backend integration through the Interceptor pattern, and master reactivity with RxJS. This section empowers developers to create dynamic and interactive experiences for their users.

In the final stretch, that is, *Part 3, Architecture and Deployment*, Alvaro delves into designing applications for testability, exploring the possibilities of micro-frontends with Angular elements, and sharing best practices for deployment. This part lays the groundwork for robust, scalable, and maintainable applications.

Finally, the *Angular Renaissance* chapter paints a vibrant picture of the future of modern Angular applications, highlighting the latest advancements and trends shaping the framework. This glimpse into the future inspires and motivates developers to stay ahead of the curve and continually improve their craft.

Alvaro's writing style is clear, concise, and engaging. He seamlessly blends theoretical concepts with practical examples, making even the most complex topics easily understandable. Additionally, his passion for Angular shines through every page, further igniting your desire to delve deeper into the framework's capabilities.

So, buckle up, fellow Angular enthusiast, and prepare to embark on a journey of knowledge and growth. With Alvaro as your guide, you'll be crafting elegant, robust, and future-proof Angular applications in no time.

Happy coding!

Loiane Groner

Published Author and Vice-President – Software Development at CitiBank

Contributors

About the author

Alvaro Camillo Neto is a software engineer, speaker, and instructor in Brazil. He has worked in the technology industry for over 10 years and is dedicated to the development of business solutions at a large company. Alvaro is a technology enthusiast, and he sees knowledge sharing as an opportunity to help the community that helped him so much and the best way of learning. He believes in technology as a tool to empower people. He has performed at small meetups and large events, focusing on the themes of developing web solutions. He also shares knowledge on his blog (`https://alvarocamillont. dev/`) and participates in the organization of AngularSP.

About the reviewer

Anu Nagan G has worked at various corporate organizations, starting at a SaaS startup (GenDeep) and moving on to midsize (GAVS) and Fortune 500 companies (DXC). There, he had various roles, such as technical product manager, full stack product lead (in Angular, Java, Python, and AWS), and delivery lead, respectively, in his 10.3 years of tenure. Currently, he is with Bounteous as a technical manager, leading global delivery projects such as migrating legacy WordPress apps to Adobe AEM. Prior to that, he led parallel projects, such as the advanced AI and analytics product CortexAI, clinical mobile app development, and Salesforce automation into B2B business. He previously contributed to various AIOps products, such as ZIF and Gcare. He is an avid reader and cinephile, loves to play guitar, and makes short films with his friends.

I would like to thank my wife and daughter, A Chekhov H, who celebrated her first birthday on 21 December, 2023.

Table of Contents

2

Organizing Your Application 21

3

TypeScript Patterns for Angular 37

4

Components and Pages 55

Part 3: Architecture and Deployment

Preface

The Angular framework has been helping development teams since 2009, with a robust structure and practically everything a web application needs. Angular, with its "batteries included" philosophy, has mechanisms for state management, route administration, and the injection of dependencies among other tools for you to create the most incredible experiences for your users.

This book aims to help you navigate this incredible list of features and learn how to orchestrate it for you and your team to get the most out of Angular and its entire ecosystem.

We will discover what types of patterns exist in the framework and what lessons we can learn from these patterns to apply to our applications.

We will also explore Angular development and architecture best practices based on its documentation, and community advice around the Angular ecosystem.

Angular is widely used by companies of different sizes and sectors. The company that sponsors this open source framework, Google, has thousands of internal applications that use Angular, guaranteeing great stability, which is one of the biggest reasons for using it.

There is a huge demand for developers who have mastered Angular and architects who can organize and get the best out of Angular, and the framework is currently in its best form, dubbed by the community as the Angular Renaissance.

Who this book is for

This book is for frontend developers and architects with experience in Angular or any other web framework who want to delve into the best that Angular can offer.

The main personas that this book is aimed toward are the following:

- Developers who already work with Angular and want to be more productive in delivering their tasks

- Technical leaders who want to bring best practices to their teams to increase the quality and productivity of their deliveries

- Software architects who want to explore the possibilities that Angular can offer applications and thus design resilient and secure systems

What this book covers

Chapter 1, Starting Projects the Right Way, reinforces the fundamentals of Angular, its principles, and how to configure your project and development environment to be as productive as possible.

Chapter 2, Organizing Your Application, explores best practices in organizing an Angular project and how to optimize your application's performance by lazy loading Angular modules.

Chapter 3, TypeScript Patterns for Angular, delves into the framework's base language, TypeScript, and helps you understand why it was chosen by the Angular team and how we can apply to our projects.

Chapter 4, Components and Pages, works with the base element of the framework, the component, and how we can structure our project to create concise and efficient applications.

Chapter 5, Angular Services and the Singleton Pattern, analyzes Angular services to separate business logic from presentation logic and best practices for communicating with the backend.

Chapter 6, Handling User Inputs: Forms, is where we will study the main way users interact with our applications, through forms, and how we can create reactive and easy-to-maintain forms.

Chapter 7, Routes and Routers, is where we will work with Angular's routing mechanism and how to manage our applications' routes in a secure and optimized way.

Chapter 8, Improving Backend Integrations: the Interceptor Pattern, is where we will apply the Interceptor design pattern to common tasks when dealing with backend communication, such as token management and user notification.

Chapter 9, Exploring Reactivity with RxJS, delves deeper into the RxJS library and how we can make the most of it for managing information flows and interactions in our projects.

Chapter 10, Design for Tests: Best Practices, discusses automated testing and how to prepare our project for this process, as well as exploring unit testing with the Jasmine and Karma libraries and end-to-end testing with the open source tool Cypress.

Chapter 11, Micro Frontend with Angular Elements, explores the micro frontend architecture and discusses when to use it and how to implement it in Angular using the Angular Elements library.

Chapter 12, Packaging Everything: Best Practices for Deployment, looks at the best practices for building and deploying our Angular applications to cloud environments. Using an example project, we will explore the Microsoft Azure cloud.

Chapter 13, The Angular Renaissance, explores how to keep ourselves and our applications up to date with the constant evolution of Angular and looks at incredible features such as Angular Signals, standalone components, and lazy loading components using the defer instruction.

To get the most out of this book

You will need to have a basic understanding of HTML, CSS, and JavaScript and how a web application works.

Software/hardware covered in the book	Operating system requirements
Angular 16 and 17	Windows, macOS, or Linux
TypeScript 5.2	
RxJS 7	
Azure	

Download the example code files

You can download the example code files for this book from GitHub at https://github.com/ PacktPublishing/Angular-Design-Patterns-and-Best-Practices. If there's an update to the code, it will be updated in the GitHub repository.

We also have other code bundles from our rich catalog of books and videos available at https:// github.com/PacktPublishing/. Check them out!

Conventions used

There are a number of text conventions used throughout this book.

Code in text: Indicates code words in text, database table names, folder names, filenames, file extensions, pathnames, dummy URLs, user input, and Twitter handles. Here is an example: "In this test case, we don't need to worry about the login because the beforeEach function performs this function and we work directly on the form."

A block of code is set as follows:

```
describe('My First Test', () => {
  it('Visits the initial project page', () => {
    cy.visit('/')
    cy.contains('app is running!')
  })
})
```

When we wish to draw your attention to a particular part of a code block, the relevant lines or items are set in bold:

```
<button
  type="submit"
  class="w-full rounded bg-blue-500 px-4 py-2 text-white"
  [disabled]="loginForm.invalid"
  [class.opacity-50]="loginForm.invalid"
  data-cy="submit"
>
  Login
</button>
```

Any command-line input or output is written as follows:

```
ng test
```

Bold: Indicates a new term, an important word, or words that you see onscreen. For instance, words in menus or dialog boxes appear in **bold**. Here is an example: "Select the desired browser and click on **Start E2E Testing** and we will have the test execution interface."

> **Tips or important notes**
> Appear like this.

Get in touch

Feedback from our readers is always welcome.

General feedback: If you have questions about any aspect of this book, email us at customercare@ packtpub.com and mention the book title in the subject of your message.

Errata: Although we have taken every care to ensure the accuracy of our content, mistakes do happen. If you have found a mistake in this book, we would be grateful if you would report this to us. Please visit www.packtpub.com/support/errata and fill in the form.

Piracy: If you come across any illegal copies of our works in any form on the internet, we would be grateful if you would provide us with the location address or website name. Please contact us at copyright@packt.com with a link to the material.

If you are interested in becoming an author: If there is a topic that you have expertise in and you are interested in either writing or contributing to a book, please visit authors.packtpub.com.

Share Your Thoughts

Once you've read *Angular Designs Patterns and Best Practices*, we'd love to hear your thoughts! Scan the QR code below to go straight to the Amazon review page for this book and share your feedback.

https://packt.link/r/1837631972

Your review is important to us and the tech community and will help us make sure we're delivering excellent quality content.

Download a free PDF copy of this book

Thanks for purchasing this book!

Do you like to read on the go but are unable to carry your print books everywhere?

Is your eBook purchase not compatible with the device of your choice?

Don't worry, now with every Packt book you get a DRM-free PDF version of that book at no cost.

Read anywhere, any place, on any device. Search, copy, and paste code from your favorite technical books directly into your application.

The perks don't stop there, you can get exclusive access to discounts, newsletters, and great free content in your inbox daily

Follow these simple steps to get the benefits:

1. Scan the QR code or visit the link below

https://packt.link/free-ebook/9781837631971

2. Submit your proof of purchase
3. That's it! We'll send your free PDF and other benefits to your email directly

Part 1: Reinforcing the Foundations

In this part you will delve deeper into the fundamentals of the Angular framework and its basic concepts such as why to use Angular, how to organize your project and set up a productive development environment. In addition, you will learn about best practices in the tasks of component creation and communication with the backend.

This part has the following chapters:

- *Chapter 1, Starting Projects the Tight Way*
- *Chapter 2, Organizing Your Application*
- *Chapter 3, TypeScript Patterns for Angular*
- *Chapter 4, Components and Pages*
- *Chapter 5, Angular Services and the Singleton Pattern*

1

Starting Projects the Right Way

Angular is a framework that has the motto "*batteries included*" as a development philosophy. This means that practically all the resources you need for your frontend application needs are already available as soon as you create a new project.

In this chapter, you will understand why choose Angular for your web application, what its main characteristics and design are, and why companies, especially the biggest ones, choose Angular as the main framework for developing single-page applications.

You will explore the technologies that make up the framework and thus take greater advantage of possible alternatives if you need them for a specific case. You'll also set up your workspace with the best tools to help you and your team's productivity.

In this chapter, we're going to cover the following topics:

- Why choose Angular?
- What technologies are present in the ecosystem?
- Configuring your development environment
- Starting an Angular project
- Using the Angular **Command-Line Interface** (**CLI**) for your productivity

By the end of this chapter, you will have arguments for using Angular in your project and be more productive in your development workspace.

Technical requirements

To follow the instructions in this chapter, you'll need the following:

- **Visual Studio Code** (**VS Code**) (https://code.visualstudio.com/Download)
- Node.js 18 or higher (https://nodejs.org/en/download/)

The code files for this chapter are available at `https://github.com/PacktPublishing/Angular-Design-Patterns-and-Best-Practices/tree/main/ch1`.

Why choose Angular?

The choice of technology to be used in a given project is critical to its success. You, as a project developer or architect, must help your team in this mission by choosing the best tool for the job.

The Angular framework is one of the most used tools for building a single-page application, along with React and Vue. When choosing the right tool for the job, you need to answer *why*.

The following are some arguments for choosing Angular.

Batteries included

Angular is an opinionated framework, which means that the Angular development team has already made several choices of tools and solutions for every challenge that a web application can have. This way, you and your team don't have to research which route engine or state management library you should use; it's all included and configured for your project.

This feature also simplifies the onboarding of new developers in your team. Following the guidelines proposed by the documentation and using the best practices, Angular projects usually have the same structure and method of development. Knowing Angular you can quickly locate yourself in any ongoing project.

Google support

Angular was created and maintained by the Angular team at Google. Although excellent frameworks such as Vue.js and Svelte are maintained only by their communities, having such a big tech company supporting the framework brings security to the choice of technology, especially for large companies.

In addition, Angular is used in more than 300 internal applications and Google products, which means stability and quality because, before each new version of the framework is released, it is validated in all these applications.

The Angular team has strived since version 13 to increase transparency within the community by releasing a roadmap (`https://angular.io/guide/roadmap`) detailing all the improvements in progress and what to expect for the future of the framework, giving you peace of mind that it will be supported for years to come.

Community

Technology is only as alive as the community that supports it, and Angular has a huge one. Meetups, podcasts, events, articles, and videos – the Angular community has many resources to help developers.

The people who make up this community also have the important contribution of giving feedback, creating and correcting issues in Angular. As it is an open source project, everyone is invited to evaluate and contribute to the code.

The Angular team also asks the community for help with major framework decisions through **Requests for Comment (RFCs)**.

In addition, the community creates many libraries that expand the possibilities of the framework, such as NgRx (`https://ngrx.io/`) for advanced state management and Transloco (`https://ngneat.github.io/transloco/`) to support internationalization, among others.

Tooling

One of the differentiating factors of Angular compared to its competitors is the focus from the beginning on tooling and developer experience. The Angular CLI tool is a powerful productivity tool that we will explore in this chapter, which is used far beyond the simple creation and setup of a project.

From a testing point of view, Angular is already equipped and configured with Karma as a test runner and Jasmine as a configuration tool. Angular's tooling already configures the project build using webpack and already has a dev server.

The tool is also extensible, allowing the community to create routines for configuring and updating their libraries.

With these arguments, you will be able to base your choice of Angular on your project; let's see now which technologies make up the framework's ecosystem.

What technologies are present in the ecosystem?

The Angular team, when creating the solution for the growing complexity of web application development, decided to unite the best tools and libraries in an opinionated package with the maximum number of configurations made by default.

We then have the following libraries that make up the core of Angular.

TypeScript

TypeScript is a superset of the JavaScript language that adds type checking and other features to the language, ensuring a better developer experience and security for web development.

It has been present in Angular since its first version and is the cornerstone of the framework that enables several features such as dependency injection, typed forms and Angular's tooling.

TypeScript is currently the preferred tool for backend development in Node.js and is encouraged by communities of other frameworks such as React and Vue.js.

RXJS

RXJS is a library that implements the reactive paradigm (`https://www.reactivemanifesto.org/`) in the JavaScript language.

Since the first version of Angular, reactivity was a core theme that the framework wanted to achieve and so it uses the **RXJS** library to help with it.

HTTP requests, routes, forms, and other Angular elements use the concepts of observables and their operators to provide Angular developers with the tools to create more fluid and dynamic applications with less boilerplate code.

RXJS also provides mechanisms for state management in a frontend application without the need to use more complex patterns such as Redux.

Karma and Jasmine

Quality should be the top priority in any application and this is especially important in frontend applications as for the user, it is *the* application.

One of the ways to attest to quality is through testing, and with that in mind, Angular already comes by default with the tool duo of **Jasmine** and **Karma**.

Jasmine is a framework for unit-testing JavaScript and TypeScript applications with several functions for assertion and test assembly.

Karma is the test runner, that is, the environment where the unit test setup is executed with the help of Jasmine. This environment, configured in its configuration file, runs in browsers, making the test more realistic in comparison to customers' daily lives.

Many people in the community switch these tools for the Jest framework due to performance in the execution of the tests, which is totally fine and even facilitated by the Angular CLI; however, it should be noted that this tool does not run in a browser, which really improves the performance of the test execution but may hide some particularity that only testing in a browser would provide.

Webpack

After the development of an application, it is necessary to create the bundle to send it to production, and Webpack is the tool that the Angular team chose for this task.

Webpack is a very powerful and versatile bundler, and it is thanks to it that the framework manages to make some interesting optimizations such as tree shaking and lazy loading of bundles.

However, Webpack is complex in its configuration, and with that in mind, the Angular team has already set up and created some abstractions for fine-tuning the tool, such as the `angular.json` file.

We understand what pieces make up the framework and how they relate to delivering rich and fluid interfaces. We will now set up our development environment.

Configuring your development environment

A well-organized environment with the right tools is the first step toward excellence and productivity; now, let's set this environment up in your workspace.

After installing Node.js following the instructions in the *Technical requirements* section, the following tools and their plugins will help you in your workflow.

VS Code

VS Code (`https://code.visualstudio.com/`) is currently the default tool for most developers, especially for frontend projects.

There are other very good ones such as WebStorm (`https://www.jetbrains.com/webstorm`), but VS Code, with its plugins especially for Angular projects, facilitates great productivity and ergonomics.

To install the plugins listed here, in the code editor, click on **Extensions** or use the shortcut *Ctrl + Shift + X* (Windows) or *Cmd + Shift + X* (macOS).

The following are the VS Code plugins recommended for developing Angular applications.

Git Extension Pack

Git Extension Pack (`https://marketplace.visualstudio.com/items?itemName=donjayamanne.git-extension-pack`) is not specifically for developing Angular applications but it is useful for any kind of work.

Git is the default tool for version control and VS Code has native support for it. This set of plugins improves this support even further, adding the ability to read comments and changes made in previous commits in the editor, support for multiple projects, and a better view of your repository history and logs.

Angular Language Service

The **Angular Language Service** (`https://marketplace.visualstudio.com/items?itemName=Angular.ng-template`) extension is maintained by the Angular team and adds support for most of the framework's functionality right from the code editor.

By adding this extension to your editor, it will have the following features:

- Autocomplete in the HTML template file, allowing you to use component methods without having to consult the TypeScript file
- Checking for possible compilation errors in HTML template files and TypeScript files

- Quick navigation between HTML and TypeScript templates, allowing you to consult the definition of methods and objects

This extension is also available for other IDEs such as WebStorm and Eclipse.

Prettier

Prettier (`https://marketplace.visualstudio.com/items?itemName=esbenp.prettier-vscode`) is a JavaScript tool that solves the code formatting problem. It is opinionated on formatting settings although some customization is possible.

In addition to TypeScript, Prettier formats HTML, CSS, JSON, and JavaScript files, making this extension useful also for backend development using Node.js.

To standardize formatting across your entire team, you can install Prettier as a package for your project and run it on the project's CI/CD track, which we'll see in *Chapter 12, Packaging Everything – Best Practices for Deployment*.

ESLint

When creating an application, the use of a linter is highly recommended to ensure good language practices and avoid errors from the beginning of development.

In the past, the default tool for linting TypeScript projects was **TSLint**, but the project has been absorbed by **ESLint** (`https://marketplace.visualstudio.com/items?itemName=dbaeumer.vscode-eslint`), which allows you to verify JavaScript and TypeScript projects.

With this extension, verification occurs quickly while you type the code of your project. ESLint can be installed as a package in your Angular project and thus performs this validation on the CI/CD conveyor of your project, which we will see in *Chapter 12, Packaging Everything – Best Practices for Deployment*.

EditorConfig

The **EditorConfig** (`https://marketplace.visualstudio.com/items?itemName=EditorConfig.EditorConfig`) plugin has the function of creating a default configuration file for not only VS Code but also any IDE that supports this format.

This plugin is useful for standardizing things for your project and your team – for example, the number of spaces that each *Tab* key represents, or whether your project will use single quotes or double quotes to represent strings.

To use it, just create or have a file named `.editorconfig` at the root of your project and VS Code will respect the settings described in the file.

VS Code settings

VS Code, in addition to extensions, has several native settings that can help in your day-to-day work. By accessing the **File** menu, we can activate the automatic saving flag so you don't have to worry about pressing *Ctrl + S* all the time (although this habit is already engraved in stone in our brains...).

Another interesting setting is **Zen** mode, where all windows and menus are hidden so you can just focus on your code. To activate it, go to **View** | **Appearance** | **Zen Mode**, or use the keyboard shortcut *Ctrl + K + Z* for Windows/Linux systems and *Cmd + K + Z* for macOS.

To improve the readability of your code during editing, an interesting setting is **Bracket coloring**, which will give each parenthesis and bracket in your code a different color.

To enable this setting, open the `configuration` file using the shortcut *Ctrl + Shift + P* for Windows/Linux or *Cmd + Shift + P* for macOS and type `Open User Settings (JSON)`.

In the file, add the following elements:

```
{
    "editor.bracketPairColorization.enabled": true,
    "editor.guides.bracketPairs": true
}
```

VS Code also has the **Inlay Hints** feature, which shows details of parameter types and return methods, as well as other useful information on the line you are reading in the code.

To configure it in the **Settings** menu, look for **Inlay Hints** and activate it if it is not already configured. For the development of your Angular application, you can also perform specific configurations by selecting **TypeScript**.

It is also possible to turn on this functionality by directly configuring the `settings.json` file with the following elements:

```
{
    "typescript.inlayHints.parameterNames.enabled": "all",
    "typescript.inlayHints.functionLikeReturnTypes.enabled": true,
    "typescript.inlayHints.parameterTypes.enabled": true,
    "typescript.inlayHints.propertyDeclarationTypes.enabled": true,
    "typescript.inlayHints.variableTypes.enabled": true,
    "editor.inlayHints.enabled": "on"
}
```

Fira Code font and ligatures

An important detail that not every developer pays attention to is the type of font they use in their code editor. A confusing font can make it difficult to read code and tire your eyes.

The ideal option is to use monospaced fonts, that is, fonts where the characters occupy the same horizontal space.

A very popular font is **Fira Code** (`https://github.com/tonsky/FiraCode`), which, in addition to being monospaced, has ligatures for programming – that is, joining or changing characters that represent symbols such as ==, >=, and =>, as shown in the following figure:

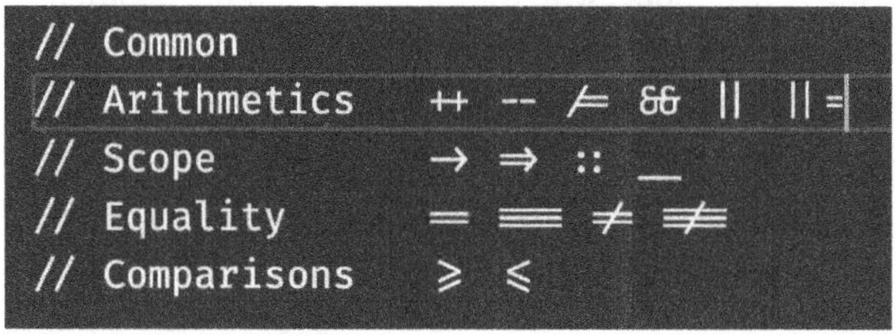

Figure 1.1 – Example of symbols with font ligatures

After installing the font on your operating system, to enable ligatures in the font in VS Code, access the `configuration` file as in the previous section and add the following elements:

```
{
    "editor.fontFamily": "Fira Code",
    "editor.fontLigatures": true,
}
```

Standardizing the extensions and settings in the project

In the *Why choose Angular?* section, we learned that one of the advantages of choosing this framework for your project is the standardization it provides to development and the team.

You can also standardize your VS Code settings and record them in your Git repository so that not only you but also our team can have that leap in productivity.

To do this, in your repository, create a folder called `.vscode`, and inside that folder, create two files. The `extensions.json` file will have all the extensions recommended by the project. In this example, we will use the extensions we saw earlier:

```
{
    "recommendations": [
        "dbaeumer.vscode-eslint",
        "esbenp.prettier-vscode",
        "Angular.ng-template",
        "donjayamanne.git-extension-pack",
        "editorconfig.editorconfig"
    ]
}
```

Let's also create the `settings.json` file, which allows you to add VS Code settings to your workspace. These settings take precedence over user settings and VS Code's default settings.

This file will have the previously suggested settings:

```
{
    "editor.bracketPairColorization.enabled": true,
    "editor.guides.bracketPairs": true
    "editor.fontFamily": "Fira Code",
    "editor.fontLigatures": true,
    "typescript.inlayHints.parameterNames.enabled": "all",
    "typescript.inlayHints.functionLikeReturnTypes.enabled": true,
    "typescript.inlayHints.parameterTypes.enabled": true,
    "typescript.inlayHints.propertyDeclarationTypes.enabled": true,
    "typescript.inlayHints.variableTypes.enabled": true,
    "editor.inlayHints.enabled": "on"
}
```

By synchronizing these files in your repository, when your team members download the project and open VS Code for the first time, the following message will appear:

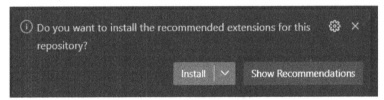

Figure 1.2 – VS Code prompt for recommended extensions

Once confirmed, all the extensions configured in the file will be installed in the VS Code development environment of your team members, thus automating the task of standardizing the team's work environment.

Angular DevTools

One tool missing from the Angular framework was a way to drill down into an application in the browser. Browsers such as Chrome and Firefox have greatly improved the developer experience over the years, broadly for all types of websites.

With that in mind, the Angular team, starting from version 12, created the Angular DevTools extension for Chrome and Firefox.

To install it, you need to go to the extension store of the browser (Chrome or Firefox) and click on **Install**.

With it installed, access to the site built with Angular, and with the build set up for development, the **Angular** tab will appear in the developer tools:

Figure 1.3 – Angular DevTools Chrome extension example

This tool allows you to browse the structure of your app, locate the code of the components on the screen, and profile your application to detect possible performance problems.

Now you have a productive development environment for developing Angular applications, we are ready to start our application.

Starting an Angular project

We have our tools installed and configured and now we are going to start our Angular application. First, we are going to install the Angular CLI, which will be responsible for creating and building our application. In your terminal, type the following command:

```
npm install -g @angular/cli@16
```

After installing the CLI, use the following command to confirm the installation:

```
ng version
```

The following figure should appear in your terminal (the Angular version may be newer):

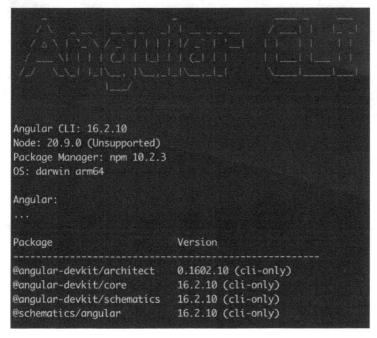

```
Angular CLI: 16.2.10
Node: 20.9.0 (Unsupported)
Package Manager: npm 10.2.3
OS: darwin arm64

Angular:
...

Package                          Version
------------------------------------------------------------
@angular-devkit/architect     0.1602.10 (cli-only)
@angular-devkit/core          16.2.10 (cli-only)
@angular-devkit/schematics    16.2.10 (cli-only)
@schematics/angular           16.2.10 (cli-only)
```

Figure 1.4 – Angular CLI prompt confirming you have correctly installed the tool

If the ng command is not recognized, restart the terminal. This ng command is the CLI call and will be used in this and other chapters of the book.

Let's start our project using the ng new command. The Angular CLI will ask for some definitions of your project:

1. The first is the name of the project; for this example, enter angular-start.

2. The second prompt is whether you'd like to configure your project's routing, for which we'll input Yes. This request will tell the CLI to create the base files for the route, which is recommended for most applications; an exception could be an Angular library you would like to create.

3. The next prompt will tell you which CSS format your project will use. Angular by default supports conventional CSS and the SCSS, Sass, and Less tools. For this and other examples in the book, we will use CSS.

4. Confirming the Angular CLI will create the entire initial structure of the project and will install the dependencies using the npm i command, leaving everything ready for the start of development, as in the following example.

```
PS C:\dev\angular-design-patterns\ch1> ng new
? What name would you like to use for the new workspace and initial project? angular-start
? Would you like to add Angular routing? Yes
? Which stylesheet format would you like to use? CSS
CREATE angular-start/angular.json (2735 bytes)
CREATE angular-start/package.json (1044 bytes)
CREATE angular-start/README.md (1066 bytes)
CREATE angular-start/tsconfig.json (901 bytes)
CREATE angular-start/.editorconfig (274 bytes)
CREATE angular-start/.gitignore (548 bytes)
CREATE angular-start/tsconfig.app.json (263 bytes)
CREATE angular-start/tsconfig.spec.json (273 bytes)
CREATE angular-start/.vscode/extensions.json (130 bytes)
CREATE angular-start/.vscode/launch.json (474 bytes)
CREATE angular-start/.vscode/tasks.json (938 bytes)
CREATE angular-start/src/favicon.ico (948 bytes)
CREATE angular-start/src/index.html (298 bytes)
CREATE angular-start/src/main.ts (214 bytes)
CREATE angular-start/src/styles.css (80 bytes)
CREATE angular-start/src/assets/.gitkeep (0 bytes)
CREATE angular-start/src/app/app-routing.module.ts (245 bytes)
CREATE angular-start/src/app/app.module.ts (393 bytes)
CREATE angular-start/src/app/app.component.html (23115 bytes)
CREATE angular-start/src/app/app.component.spec.ts (1094 bytes)
CREATE angular-start/src/app/app.component.ts (217 bytes)
CREATE angular-start/src/app/app.component.css (0 bytes)
✓ Packages installed successfully.
```

Figure 1.5 – Prompt of files generated by angular-cli

To verify that the project was successfully installed, in your operating system's terminal, type the following command:

```
ng serve
```

This command will start the development web server and load the example project page, as shown in *Figure 1.6*:

Figure 1.6 – Example page generated by angular-cli on project creation

The `ng new` command has other options that can be used for specific needs in your project. They are listed in the official documentation (`https://angular.io/cli/new`), and here are some that may be interesting:

- Parameter `'—package-manager'`: With this parameter, it is possible to choose another node package manager such as **yarn** (`https://yarnpkg.com/`).

- Parameter `'--skip-install'`: With this parameter, the CLI does not perform the package installation step, which can be useful for creating automation tools for your team.

- Parameter `'--strict'`: This parameter is set to `true` by default, but it is important to mention it because it configures your project in `strict` mode, which configures the TypeScript and Angular mechanisms to improve type and template validations. For more details, see *Chapter 3, TypeScript Patterns for Angular.*

Project structure

The Angular CLI creates the project in the structure recommended by the Angular team with all files configured by default. To deepen our knowledge of the framework, we need to know the main files, their functions, and available customizations as follows:

- `src`: This is the folder where your project will be, including all components, modules, and services.

- `assets`: Contains the static files you will need in your project, such as images and icons. In the build process, by default, it will export the files from this folder without any changes to the production build.

- `index.html`: This is the initial file of your application. This file will be used in the build process, and it is recommended not to change it unless there is a very specific need. The title information must be changed with an Angular feature and not directly in this file.

- `main.ts`: This is the first JavaScript file that will be loaded in your application. You shouldn't change it unless your project has a very specific need for it to be changed.

- `styles.css`: This is the file that can contain the global CSS of your application, that is, the CSS that can be read by all components since Angular by default isolates the CSS of each component. This file is usually modified when your project uses a design system such as Material (`https://material.angular.io/`).

- `.editorconfig`: As described in the *VS Code* section of this chapter, this file, together with the extension that interprets and configures the IDE, allows standardization in your code conventions, such as the use of double or single quotes and the use of tabs or indentation spaces.

- `angular.json`: This is the most important configuration file for an Angular application. In it, you can customize the way your project is built, and define *budgets* for the size of bundles (more details in *Chapter 12, Packaging Everything – Best Practices for Deployment*), among other settings.

- `package.json` and `package-lock.json`: These files refer to the dependencies of the npm packages of your project and also the place to create the npm scripts that will be used in the creation of the CI/CD pipes of the Angular application (more details in *Chapter 12, Packaging Everything – Best Practices for Deployment*).

As of version 15 of Angular, the CLI hides Karma configuration files and environment variables files (`enviroment.ts`) by default with the justification of simplifying the project structure. It is still possible to create these files for fine-tuning your application build, test, and environment processes (more details in *Chapter 8, Improving Backend Integrations: the Interceptor Pattern*).

We created our project using the `angular-cli` tool, but this tool can help us even more, as we will learn next.

Using the Angular CLI for your productivity

We learned how to create a project with all its options, but the Angular CLI is far from being just a project creation tool. It is a very important tool for the productivity and workflow of an Angular application. All available options are described using the following command:

```
ng --help
```

We will detail some of the most interesting options here, and in the next chapters, we will continue to use them, given the practicality of this tool.

ng add

This command has the function of adding an Angular library to your project. You might be wondering, *Doesn't npm install do the same thing?* and you'd be right. However, when you need to install Angular Material as a library, installing the dependency is just the first step.

Many libraries such as Angular Material itself need the configuration of the `angular.json` file and the creation of some other `lib` file, among other tasks. The `ng add` command allows the library creator to automate these steps and simplify their workflow.

To exemplify this in the project that we created, we will use the following command:

```
ng add @angular/material
```

Executing the preceding command, the library will make some prompts (in the same format as we saw for the `ng new` command) and in the end, it will configure our project with the library, as shown in *Figure 1.7*.

```
PS C:\dev\angular-design-patterns\ch1\angular-start> ng add @angular/material
i Using package manager: npm
✓ Found compatible package version: @angular/material@15.0.3.
✓ Package information loaded.

The package @angular/material@15.0.3 will be installed and executed.
Would you like to proceed? Yes
✓ Packages successfully installed.
? Choose a prebuilt theme name, or "custom" for a custom theme: Purple/Green         [ Preview: https://material.angular.io?theme=purple-green ]
? Set up global Angular Material typography styles? Yes
? Include the Angular animations module? Include and enable animations
UPDATE package.json (1110 bytes)
✓ Packages installed successfully.
UPDATE src/app/app.module.ts (502 bytes)
UPDATE angular.json (2943 bytes)
UPDATE src/index.html (580 bytes)
UPDATE src/styles.css (181 bytes)
```

Figure 1.7 – Installation of Angular Material using angular-cli

ng update

In the development of our projects, updating the version of something often takes more time than adding a new library. The ng update command makes this task almost trivial, being one of the greatest allies when it comes to updating the Angular version of our application.

On the Angular update website (https://update.angular.io/), the Angular team details how to update a project in old versions. Larger and more complex projects may have their quirks (which are usually described on the website), but all applications start with the following command (in this case, version 15):

```
ng update @angular/core@15 @angular/cli@15
```

The Angular CLI will take care of updating the package and even making possible automation-breaking changes; often, only this is enough to completely update your application.

This command, like ng add, is also available for libraries that have been configured by their authors and can benefit from this automation.

ng serve

This command is used by every Angular developer (it's the first thing you should do after creating a project) and its function is to upload a development web server.

One of the most interesting and productive features of this command is the hot-reload capability; that is, the server restarts every time a project file is updated, allowing you to see its modification in real time in the interface.

A productivity tip for this command is to use the open parameter as follows:

```
ng serve --open
```

With this parameter, as soon as Angular loads your application, the CLI will open the default browser of your operating system with the application you are working on.

ng build

The `ng build` command is intended to prepare your application bundle to be executed by the production web server of your choice.

It performs a series of optimizations to guarantee the delivery of the smallest possible bundle of your application.

This results in a performance gain since with a smaller bundle, your client downloads faster, which is important, especially in environments with slow internet.

We will discuss this command in more detail in *Chapter 12, Packaging Everything – Best Practices for Deployment.*

ng deploy

The `ng deploy` command allows you to fully deploy your application to a cloud provider such as Microsoft Azure.

This command works together with the Angular library of the provider you want to use, so for it to work, you need to install it.

We will discuss this command in more detail in *Chapter 12, Packaging Everything – Best Practices for Deployment.*

ng generate

The `ng generate` command has the function to generate almost all types of Angular components that your application can use. This function brings a productivity gain in your workflow as it generates all the necessary files.

Let's generate our `about` page in our example project with the following command:

```
ng generate component about
```

We can analyze in our project folders that the Angular CLI created the TypeScript, HTML, and CSS files necessary for rendering the component.

However, it also generated the unit test file for this component and updated the module for its use. All these files already have the minimum boilerplate for the development of the component.

In addition to generating practically all standard Angular components, this command can be used by external libraries that want to provide this development experience, as in the following example of Angular Material:

```
ng generate @angular/material:navigation home
```

In almost every chapter of the book, we'll use this command to generate the components we're going to study and the best practices and patterns for them.

Summary

In this chapter, we covered the features and philosophy of Angular and how to start a project in the most productive way. We learned which technologies make up its ecosystem and how to configure its desktop with the best VS Code extensions and settings. Finally, we learned how to start a project with the Angular CLI and what other features this powerful tool can provide us with.

Now you'll be able to argue why to use Angular in your team's project and you'll be able to help it set up a productive work environment. You'll also be able to use the Angular CLI to create and maintain your project.

In the next chapter, we will learn how to organize the components of an Angular application.

2

Organizing Your Application

A messed-up project is a bug's nest waiting to spoil your user experience. In addition to quality, good organization of your project from the beginning will give your team productivity and, in the case of Angular, potential improvement in the performance of your application.

In this chapter, you will learn about the function of Angular modules, the difference between these and JavaScript modules, and how to use them in the best way for your project.

You will learn about the single module app anti-pattern and how and why to avoid it. You will also use Angular modules to optimize the import of common components to your application using the `SharedModule` pattern. Finally, you will understand how to use lazy loading to optimize your application's performance.

In this chapter, we're going to cover the following topics:

- Organizing the application with Angular modules
- The first module: `AppModule`
- Avoiding anti-pattern: single module app
- Optimizing the usage of common modules: the `SharedModule` pattern
- Improving the size of your app: lazy loading

By the end of this chapter, you will be able to organize your Angular application into functional and optimized modules.

Technical requirements

To follow the instructions in this chapter, you'll need the following:

- Visual Studio Code (`https://code.visualstudio.com/Download`)
- Node.js 18 or higher (`https://nodejs.org/en/download/`)

The code files for this chapter are available at `https://github.com/PacktPublishing/Angular-Design-Patterns-and-Best-Practices/tree/main/ch2`.

Organizing the application with Angular modules

The basis for organizing the components of an application using the framework is the Angular modules, more recognized in the documentation and the community by the name **NgModules**.

An Angular module is a TypeScript class marked with the @NgModule decorator that contains metadata, as in this example:

```
import { NgModule } from '@angular/core';
@NgModule({
  declarations: [SimulationComponent],
  providers:[],
  imports: [
    CommonModule,
    SharedModule,
    MatCardModule,
    MatButtonModule,
    MatSelectModule,
    MatRadioModule,ReactiveFormsModule,
  ],
  exports: [SimulationComponent],
})
export class SimulationModule {}
```

Let's detail each of these types of metadata in the following subsections.

declarations

This metadata contains an array of components, directives, and pipes that make up the module. These components must belong to only one module, otherwise, the Angular compiler will throw an error, as shown in *Figure 2.1*:

```
Error: src/app/home/home.component.ts:9:14 - error NG6007: The Component 'HomeComponent' is declared by more th
n one NgModule.

9  export class HomeComponent implements OnInit {

  src/app/simulation/simulation.module.ts:10:38
    10    declarations: [SimulationComponent,HomeComponent],

  'HomeComponent' is listed in the declarations of the NgModule 'SimulationModule'.
  src/app/home/home.module.ts:10:18
    10    declarations: [HomeComponent],

  'HomeComponent' is listed in the declarations of the NgModule 'HomeModule'.
```

Figure 2.1 – Error message when declaring a component in more than one module

providers

In this attribute, we can register the classes we want to inject using Angular's dependency injector system, normally used for services (which will be detailed in *Chapter 5, Angular Services and the Singleton Pattern*.

imports

In this metadata, we inform the modules that we want to import and use their components and services. For example, if we want to use Angular's HTTP request services, we must declare the `HttpClientModule` module here.

It is important to know that, here, we should not import components or services, only Ngmodules.

exports

By default, all items in the `declarations` attribute are private. This means that if a module contains the `StateSelectorComponent` component and another module, for example, importing the module to use this component will cause the following error to occur:

```
Error: src/app/simulation/simulation/simulation.component.html:10:13 - error NG8001: 'app-states-selector' is not a known ele
ment:
1. If 'app-states-selector' is an Angular component, then verify that it is part of this module.
2. If 'app-states-selector' is a Web Component then add 'CUSTOM_ELEMENTS_SCHEMA' to the '@NgModule.schemas' of this component
to suppress this message.

        <app-states-selector></app-states-selector>

  src/app/simulation/simulation/simulation.component.ts:6:16
    templateUrl: './simulation.component.html',

  Error occurs in the template of component SimulationComponent.
```

Figure 2.2 – Error message when using a component not exported correctly

To inform Angular that the component can be used, it is necessary to declare it in the `exports` metadata.

Unlike the `imports` metadata, here, you can declare components, pipes, directives, and other modules (as we'll see in the *Optimizing the usage of common modules – the SharedModule pattern* section).

Now that we know how to declare a module, let's study the module that is generated when creating an Angular project.

The first module – AppModule

The modules in Angular are so important to the framework that when you start a project, it automatically creates a module called **AppModule**.

This module contains all the parameters we studied in the previous section (`declarations`, `providers`, `imports`, and `exports`), plus one additional parameter: `bootstrap`. This module contains the first component to be injected into the application's `index.html` file and will be the root of your Angular application's component tree.

You may be wondering which `index.html` file and which tree this is.

As we described in *Chapter 1*, *Starting Projects the Right Way*, Angular is a framework for **single-page applications (SPAs)**, and the `index.html` file is in fact the only *page* delivered by the web server to its user.

All interfaces rendered by the Angular engine (called **Ivy**) are built from this `index.html` file and the first component is described in the `bootstrap` metadata. This rendering obeys a data structure of the logical tree type, and the root of this tree is this first component.

What is the difference between Angular and JavaScript modules?

Almost all programming languages offer a way for their developers to organize functions, classes, and variables in one or more files, allowing greater maintainability and separation of concerns.

In JavaScript, sometime after its creation and several proposals, the concept of language modules was consolidated. The best way to explain this concept is to demonstrate it with an example. First, we create a `sum.mjs` file – the `sum` function that receives two numbers and returns their sum. The important thing here is that we use the `export` keyword to indicate that we want to use it in a scope outside of its source file:

```
export function sum(numberA, numberB) {
  return numberA + numberB;
}
```

In the `index.mjs` file, we will use the created function and, for that, we make the declaration in the first line of the file. Using the reserved word `import`, we indicate which function and which file it is from:

```
import {sum} from './sum.mjs';

const numberA = 5;
const numberB = 10;

console.log(sum(numberA,numberB));
```

You may be wondering why the `.mjs` extension is used. It's because, in the example, we are using Node.js to execute, and this type of module – **ECMAScript modules (ESM)**, as the official name of the Javascript language is ECMAScript – was introduced in version 14.

Angular, as well as all other SPA frameworks, uses JavaScript modules in its development, and we can notice in any Angular component or service that we export the classes and import using the ESM:

```
import { Component } from '@angular/core';

@Component({
  selector: 'app-home',
  templateUrl: './home.component.html',
  styleUrls: ['./home.component.css']
})
export class HomeComponent {
```

In the preceding code snippet, we are importing the `Component` decorator from the `@angular/core` library and exporting the `HomeComponent` class to use in other parts of our project.

Modules type

Now that we understand and have reinforced the concept of modules in the Angular framework, let's divide our application and make better use of this feature. There is no fixed rule for organizing the modules of an application, but the Angular team and the community suggest the separation of modules based on the grouping of functionalities with common characteristics.

Based on this thought, we can have the following types of Angular modules:

- Business domain modules
- Component modules

Business domain modules

An application will serve one or more user workflows. This type of module aims to group these flows based on the affinity of the interfaces that compose them. For example, in an application for resource management, we can have the accounting module and the inventory module.

In the application available in the ch2 folder, there is the *talktalk* application that we will use in this and other chapters to put our knowledge into practice. In the project folder, let's create the home module with the following command:

```
ng g m home
```

In this command, we use the Angular CLI, ng, and the abbreviations g for **generate** and m for **module**. Then we give the name of the module, home.

Let's create the Page component that will represent the application's home page and, since we are using Angular material, we will use the Angular CLI to generate a page with a side menu using the following command:

```
ng generate @angular/material:navigation home/home
```

The Angular CLI, besides creating the component, also edited the home.module.ts file by adding it to the declarations attribute. Change this file as shown in the following example:

```
import { NgModule } from '@angular/core';
import { CommonModule } from '@angular/common';
import { HomeComponent } from './home/home.component';
import { LayoutModule } from '@angular/cdk/layout';
import { MatToolbarModule } from '@angular/material/toolbar';
import { MatButtonModule } from '@angular/material/button';
import { MatSidenavModule } from '@angular/material/sidenav';
import { MatIconModule } from '@angular/material/icon';
import { MatListModule } from '@angular/material/list';

@NgModule({
  declarations: [HomeComponent],
  imports: [
    CommonModule,
    LayoutModule,
    MatToolbarModule,
    MatButtonModule,
    MatSidenavModule,
    MatIconModule,
    MatListModule,
  ],
  exports: [HomeComponent],
})
export class HomeModule {}
```

In this module, we will export the HomeComponent component to use in the application's route. In the app.module.ts file, import the module as follows:

```
import { NgModule } from '@angular/core';
import { BrowserModule } from '@angular/platform-browser';

import { AppRoutingModule } from './app-routing.module';
import { AppComponent } from './app.component';
import { BrowserAnimationsModule } from '@angular/platform-browser/
animations';
import { HomeModule } from './home/home.module';

@NgModule({
 declarations: [
   AppComponent
 ],
 imports: [
   BrowserModule,
   AppRoutingModule,
   BrowserAnimationsModule,
   HomeModule
 ],
 providers: [],
 bootstrap: [AppComponent]
})
export class AppModule { }
```

With the module in the import attribute of the NgModule metadata, we can change the route in the app-routing.module.ts file:

```
import { NgModule } from '@angular/core';
import { Routes, RouterModule } from '@angular/router';
import { HomeComponent } from './home/home/home.component';

const routes: Routes = [
  { path: '', pathMatch: 'full', redirectTo: 'home' },
  {
    path: 'home',
    component: HomeComponent
  },
];

@NgModule({
 imports: [RouterModule.forRoot(routes)],
```

```
    exports: [RouterModule],
})
export class AppRoutingModule {}
```

The `routes` component is also `NgModule`, however, it is specialized in organizing routes, and imports and exports only `RouterModule` from Angular. Here, in the `routes` array, we create the direction for HomeComponent.

Running the `ng serve --o` command, we get the application's home page:

Figure 2.3 – talktalk sample application menu page

Component modules

The purpose of this module is to group directive components and pipes that will be reused by business domain components and even other components. Even using a component library such as Angular Material, your system will need custom components according to the business rules of your business domain.

This type of component has components, directives, and pipes declared in the `declaration` attribute and exported in the `exports` attribute, as shown in the following example:

```
import { NgModule } from '@angular/core';
import { CommonModule } from '@angular/common';
import { StatesSelectorComponent } from './states-selector/states-
selector.component';
import { MatSelectModule } from '@angular/material/select';

@NgModule({
  declarations: [StatesSelectorComponent],
  imports: [CommonModule, MatSelectModule],
  exports: [StatesSelectorComponent],
})
export class ComponentsModule {}
```

Separating the project into business domain modules and components will organize your code and improve its maintainability. Let's analyze a common anti-pattern in Angular applications.

Avoiding anti-pattern – single module app

When we are starting to study and develop with Angular, it is very common not to pay much attention to the organization and use of the application modules. As we studied at the beginning of this chapter, NgModules are so fundamental to Angular that as soon as we start a project, the Angular CLI creates the first module for the project, `AppModule`.

In theory, only this module is necessary for your application to work. From there, we can declare all the components and directives, and import all the libraries that the project might need, as we can see in the following example:

```
import { NgModule } from '@angular/core';
. . .
@NgModule({
  declarations: [
    AppComponent,
    StatesSelectorComponent,
    HomeComponent,
    SimulationComponent
  ],
  imports: [
    BrowserModule,AppRoutingModule,
    BrowserAnimationsModule,HttpClientModule,
    ReactiveFormsModule,LayoutModule,
    MatToolbarModule,MatButtonModule,
    MatSidenavModule,MatIconModule,
    MatListModule,
  ],
  bootstrap: [AppComponent]
})
export class AppModule { }
```

This approach has some problems and is an anti-pattern that we'll call a single-module app.

The problems we have here are as follows:

- **Disorganized folder structure**: The team will soon not know which components belong to which area of the project. As the project grows, this file will get bigger and more confusing.

- **Bundle size and build time**: Angular has several build and bundle optimizations that depend on the definition of application modules. Staying in just one module, these optimizations are not very effective.

- **Component maintainability and update issues**: As this file grows, the team will have difficulties deprecating no longer used components or updating those components where the Angular CLI is unable to update automatically.

The solution to this anti-pattern is to apply what we learned in this chapter: separating modules into business domain (or feature) and component modules.

We can use NgModel to reduce the repetition of importing common components in the application, as we will see in the next section about the SharedModule pattern.

Optimizing the usage of common modules – the SharedModule pattern

If we look at Angular projects, we will see patterns of use of modules such as HttpModule, as in the following example:

```
import { NgModule } from '@angular/core';
import { CommonModule } from '@angular/common';
import { HomeComponent } from './home/home.component';
import { LayoutModule } from '@angular/cdk/layout';
import { MatToolbarModule } from '@angular/material/toolbar';
import { MatButtonModule } from '@angular/material/button';
import { MatSidenavModule } from '@angular/material/sidenav';
import { MatIconModule } from '@angular/material/icon';
import { MatListModule } from '@angular/material/list';

@NgModule({
  declarations: [HomeComponent],
  imports: [
    CommonModule,
    LayoutModule,
    MatToolbarModule,
    MatButtonModule,
    MatSidenavModule,
    MatIconModule,
    MatListModule,
  ],
  exports: [HomeComponent],
})
export class HomeModule {}
```

To avoid code duplication and also make it easier for new team members, don't forget to add an important module to the project; we can create the SharedModule call to centralize the common dependencies of an Angular project.

Let's do this in our project using the Angular CLI:

```
ng generate module shared
```

In the newly generated file, we will place the Angular Material dependencies:

```
import { NgModule } from '@angular/core';
...
@NgModule({
 imports: [
   CommonModule,
   LayoutModule,
   MatToolbarModule,
   MatButtonModule,
   MatSidenavModule,
   MatIconModule,
   MatListModule,
 ],
 exports: [
   CommonModule,
   LayoutModule,
   MatToolbarModule,
   MatButtonModule,
   MatSidenavModule,
   MatIconModule,
   MatListModule,
 ]
})
export class SharedModule { }
```

In this module, we are importing Angular Material's dependencies and exporting the same dependencies, without declaring any component, directive, or pipe.

In the home.module.ts file, we can refactor to use SharedModule:

```
import { NgModule } from '@angular/core';
import { HomeComponent } from './home/home.component';
import { SharedModule } from '../shared/shared.module';

@NgModule({
 declarations: [HomeComponent],
```

```
  imports: [
    SharedModule
  ],
  exports: [HomeComponent],
})
export class HomeModule {}
```

Notice how the file has become much more succinct and easier to read using `SharedModule`.

> **Important**
>
> The modules present in `SharedModule` must be modules common to the majority of modules in your project, as this can increase the size of the module's bundle. If the module needs some specific dependency, you must declare it in that dependency and not in `SharedModule`.

In the next topic, we'll see a feature that will improve your user's experience and is based on organizing the application into modules.

Improving the size of your app – lazy loading

A good strategy for separating modules from your Angular application will increase your team's productivity and improve code organization. But another advantage that will impact the quality for your user is the use of the lazy loading technique for modules.

If we run the build process of the sample application using the `ng build` command, we can see the following message:

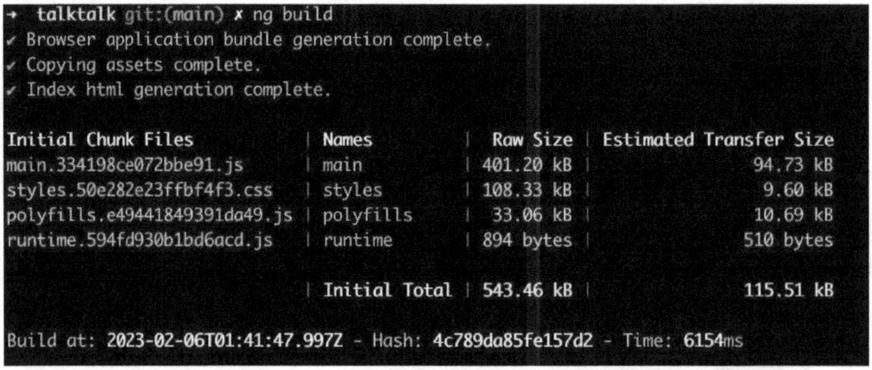

Figure 2.4 – Sample application bundle size

The size of our application's initial bundle (the `main.ts` file) is 94.73 kB, which may seem small, but for the size of our application with few features, it is a considerable size.

As the project has more features, the tendency is for this initial bundle to increase considerably, harming our users' experience as they will initially need to download a larger file. This problem particularly manifests itself in environments where the internet is not very good, such as 3G networks.

To reduce this file and consequently improve our user experience, the ideal is to have smaller packages and for these packages to be loaded only when necessary – that is, in a lazy way.

We are going to refactor our project, and the first step we have already taken is to separate the functionalities into feature modules (in the *Avoiding anti-pattern – single module app* section, we explained the danger of not separating the application modules, and without a doubt, the size of the bundle is the most impactful for the user).

Now, let's create a route file for the Home module. As the module already exists, let's manually create the `home-routing.module.ts` file in the same folder as the `home.module.ts` file.

In this file, we will add the following code:

```
import { NgModule } from '@angular/core';
import { Routes, RouterModule } from '@angular/router';
import { HomeComponent } from './home/home.component';

const routes: Routes = [
  {
    path: '',
    component: HomeComponent,
  },
];

@NgModule({
  imports: [RouterModule.forChild(routes)],
  exports: [RouterModule],
})
export class HomeRoutingModule {}
```

This route file is similar to the application's main route file, with the difference that `@NgModule`'s import uses the `forChild` method instead of `forRoot`. This is because this module is a subroute of the main route.

Another important detail to note is that the chosen path for the `HomeComponent` component is empty. We can explain this because the main route file that defines the `/home` route and how this module represents the `/home` component is already defined.

In the `home.module.ts` file, let's change it to import the route file:

```
import { NgModule } from '@angular/core';
import { HomeComponent } from './home/home.component';
import { SharedModule } from '../shared/shared.module';
import { HomeRoutingModule } from './home-routing.module';

@NgModule({
  declarations: [HomeComponent],
  imports: [
    SharedModule,HomeRoutingModule
  ]
})
export class HomeModule {}
```

In this file, we also removed the export of the `HomeComponent` component because the Home module route file will load it.

In the project's main route file, `app-routing.module.ts`, let's refactor it as follows:

```
import { NgModule } from '@angular/core';
import { Routes, RouterModule } from '@angular/router';

const routes: Routes = [
  { path: '', pathMatch: 'full', redirectTo: 'home' },
  {
    path: 'home',
    loadChildren: () =>
      import('./home/home.module').then((file) => file.HomeModule),
  },
];
@NgModule({
  imports: [RouterModule.forRoot(routes)],
  exports: [RouterModule],
})
export class AppRoutingModule {}
```

In this code, the most important part is the `loadChildren` attribute. This is where we configure the lazy load, as we pass to Angular's route mechanism a function that returns an `import` promise.

Note that the `import` function is not an Angular function, but a standard JavaScript function that allows dynamic loading of code. Angular's route engine uses this language feature to bring this functionality.

Finally, in the main module, `AppModule`, let's remove the `HomeModule` import:

```
import { NgModule } from '@angular/core';
import { BrowserModule } from '@angular/platform-browser';

import { AppRoutingModule } from './app-routing.module';
import { AppComponent } from './app.component';
import { BrowserAnimationsModule } from '@angular/platform-browser/
animations';

@NgModule({
  declarations: [
    AppComponent
  ],
  imports: [
    BrowserModule,
    AppRoutingModule,
    BrowserAnimationsModule
  ],
  providers: [],
  bootstrap: [AppComponent]
})
export class AppModule { }
```

Running our application with the `ng serve` command, we didn't notice any difference. However, when executing the `ng build` command, we can notice the following diagnosis:

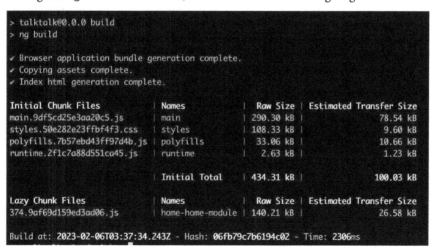

Figure 2.5 – Application bundle size after refactoring with lazy loading

The Angular build process has separated the Home module into its own bundle and the main.ts bundle has been made smaller. The difference may seem small but note that, this way, our application can scale and grow in complexity and the initial bundle will remain small or grow very little.

The new features continue to exist and be loaded by the application, but the initial loading will be faster, and these new features will be downloaded on demand only when the user accesses the route they want, giving a very positive fluidity and responsiveness.

Summary

In this chapter, we studied the Angular modules in detail and how we can use them for the organization and performance of our applications. We learned the difference between Angular modules and JavaScript modules, and we saw each attribute of a module definition and the types that we can create in the project. Finally, we learned how to avoid the single module app anti-pattern and how to create the SharedModule.

We reiterated our example application to use lazy loading of bundles, which demonstrates that good module organization reflects performance and fluidity for our users. Now, you are able to organize your application in such a way that it can scale and increase in complexity and features without compromising the maintainability of the project.

In the next chapter, we will learn how to use TypeScript effectively and productively for our Angular projects.

TypeScript Patterns for Angular

Since version 2 of the framework, Angular is based on TypeScript for its development, both internally and for those who use it to build applications.

This was a controversial decision at the time, as this JavaScript superset, created by Microsoft, was new. Nowadays, most web frameworks, such as React, Vue.js, and Svelte, support TypeScript, and some web frameworks actively recommend TypeScript as the language to use.

In this chapter, we will study the best practices and patterns for using TypeScript with Angular and beyond; these techniques can be applied to Node.js backend development and even other web frameworks, such as React and Vue.js.

We'll learn how to better declare our application's methods and functions and how to leverage TypeScript's type inference mechanism to make our classes less verbose.

In this chapter, we're going to cover the following topics:

- Creating classes and types
- Creating methods and functions
- Decreasing verbosity: type inference
- Validating types: type guards
- Using a better alternative to the any type

By the end of the chapter, you will be able to better apply TypeScript resources in your projects, improving the quality of your code and the productivity of your team.

Technical requirements

To follow the instructions in this chapter, you'll need the following:

- **Visual Studio Code (VS Code)** (https://code.visualstudio.com/Download)
- Node.js 18 or higher (https://nodejs.org/en/download/)

The code files for this chapter are available at `https://github.com/PacktPublishing/ Angular-Design-Patterns-and-Best-Practices/tree/main/ch3`.

Creating classes and types

The basis of application development using Angular is object-oriented programming, so it is important for us to delve into how to create classes and instantiate objects. Using TypeScript instead of pure JavaScript, we have another powerful element in our toolbox of types.

By typifying variables and objects, the TypeScript transpiler is able to carry out checks and alerts, preventing errors that could occur at runtime during development if this process did not exist.

Bear in mind that after transpiling (a process that transforms TypeScript code into JavaScript), the code delivered to the client's browser is pure JavaScript, including some optimizations; that is, code written in TypeScript is no less performant than code written directly in JavaScript.

To start with the fundamentals, let's explore primitive and basic types.

Primitive and basic types

JavaScript, despite not being a strongly typed language, has three types called primitives:

- `boolean`: Represents the two binary values `false` and `true`
- `string`: Represents a set of characters such as words
- `number`: Represents numerical values

For each of these primitive types, TypeScript already has a datatype that represents them, namely, `Boolean`, `String`, and `Number`, respectively.

> **Important**
>
> The first letter of the primitive types in TypeScript is in uppercase to differentiate it from the primitive JavaScript types. If you want to check a type at runtime using the `typeof` function, use the names of the primitives in lowercase.

To declare the variables of these types, just use the `:` symbol in front of the variable declaration, as in the following example:

```
export function primitive_example() {
  let name: string;
  let age: number;
  let isAlive: boolean;

  name = "Mario";
```

```
  age = 9;
  isAlive = true;

  console.log(`Name:${name} Age:${age} is alive:${isAlive ? "yes" :
"no"}`);
}
```

In the preceding example, we declare the `name`, `age`, and `isAlive` variables as `string`, `number`, and `boolean`, respectively. Note that we can use JavaScript type names in TypeScript because TypeScript allows both forms for these primitive types.

In JavaScript, it is very common to use the array data structure. This structure allows us to store and manipulate a list of values for our applications. TypeScript has a type for this structure called `Array`, where it is possible not only to create a variable with that type but also to typify what kind of values the array will contain:

```
export function array_example() {
  let names: Array<string>;
  let surnames: string[];

  names = ["Mario", "Gabriel", "Lucy"];
  surnames = ["Camillo", "Smith"];

  names.forEach((name) => console.log(`Name:${name}`));
  surnames.forEach((surname) => console.log(`Surname:${surname}`));
}
```

In this function, we declare the `names` array using the `Array` type and declare that it is a `string` list because we are informing it between square braquets.. In the `surnames` array declaration, we make the same declaration but use a TypeScript syntax sugar using `[]` after the `string` type. This way of declaring has the same effect; it's just more succinct.

At the end of the example, we use `Array`'s `foreach` method to print the elements of the array. Finally, another basic type that is widely used is the `any` type. This type tells the TypeScript transpiler not to perform any type checking on it, and its content can be type-changed anywhere in the code, as in the following example:

```
export function any_example(){
  let information:any;
  information = 'Mario';
  console.log(`Name: ${information}`);
  information = 7;
  console.log(`Age: ${information}`);
}
```

The `information` variable is declared as `any` and then we put the `Mario` string in it. We subsequently redefine the variable with the value 5.

By default, in TypeScript, every variable that does not have its type declared, or that has its value defined in its declaration, is of type `any`.

This language rule allows, for example, a project with JavaScript code to be incrementally converted to TypeScript by initially declaring all variables of the `any` type. Another use of the `any` type is when your code needs the flexibility of JavaScript for some more general algorithm types.

However, it is recommended that Angular developers avoid using `any` because it partially disables the checks that TypeScript performs in your code, without taking advantage of its power.

We'll see alternatives throughout the chapter, should you need the flexibility of the `any` type, without sacrificing type checking and TypeScript inference.

Classes

Building on our knowledge of basic types, let's now create more complex data types. The first one we're going to explore is **classes**. An essential element of object-oriented programming, the class represents a model, which can be real, such as a person or vehicle, or abstract, such as a text box on a web page.

From the class, we create the objects that are the elements that our systems will manipulate to execute a business rule, as in the following example:

```
class Person {
  name: string;
  age: number;

  constructor(name: string, age: number) {
    this.name = name;
    this.age = age;
  }
}

export function basic_class() {
  let client: Person = new Person("Mario", 7);
  console.log(`Name:${client.name} Age:${client.age}`);
}
```

First, we declare the `Person` class with the `name` and `age` properties by typing the properties, and then we create a method for the class called `constructor`. This method is special because it defines the rule for how the object will be instantiated from this class.

In the `basic_class` function, we instantiate an object called `client`, which is of the `Person` type with the `new` keyword. To retrieve the properties of this instantiated object, we use the notation `client.name` and `client.age`.

This declaration and use of class in TypeScript is almost the same as JavaScript except for typing the attributes of the class.

The same example in pure JavaScript would be as follows:

```javascript
class Person {
  constructor(name, age) {
    this.name = name;
    this.age = age;
  }
}
function basic_class() {
  let client = new Person("Mario", 7);
  console.log(`Name:${client.name} Age:${client.age}`);
}
```

Notice that the process of declaring the class and instantiating an object from it changes very little from TypeScript. However, as we will see in the following code block, TypeScript provides more resources for the use of the class in our projects.

In addition to attributes, classes also define methods, which are functions that an object can perform. In the example we are working on, we are now going to add a method:

```typescript
class Person {
  name: string;
  age: number;

  constructor(name: string, age: number) {
    this.name = name;
    this.age = age;
  }

  toString(){
    return `Name:${this.name} Age:${this.age}`;
  }
}
```

The `toString` method returns a `string` that represents the object, so it accesses the attribute of the object instance using the reserved JavaScript word `this`.

There is a concept in object-oriented programming called the **encapsulation of attributes**. This consists of defining which attributes are accessible to the function that instantiates a given object.

This concept, important for the correct use of some design patterns, does not exist in its entirety in JavaScript. Every class attribute is public, but in TypeScript it is implemented and validated by the transpiler, as in the following example:

```
class Person {
  name: string;
  age: number;
  private id:number;

  constructor(name: string, age: number) {
    this.name = name;
    this.age = age;
    this.id =Math.floor(Math.random() * 1000);
  }

  toString(){
    return `Name:${this.name} Age:${this.age} ID: ${this.id}`;
  }
}
```

Here, we create a property called id that is generated when the object is instantiated, and we use the reserved word private, indicating that it should not be accessed from outside the class. Note that in class methods, this attribute is accessed normally.

Let's try to force access from outside as in the following example to see what happens:

```
export function basic_class() {
  let client: Person = new Person("Mario", 7);
  console.log(client.toString());
  client.id = 100;
}
```

In this function, we instantiate a client object of the Person class and then we try to modify the id attribute. When trying to run the code, the TypeScript will indicate the following error:

```
TSError: × Unable to compile TypeScript:
src/basic_types/classes_basic.ts:21:10 - error TS2341: Property 'id' is private and
only accessible within class 'Person'.
21    client.id = 100;
```

Figure 3.1 – Error message when accessing a private attribute

Another object-oriented programming concept is inheritance. It defines an *is a* relationship between classes, as in, *a customer is a person*.

In practice, it makes a class have all the attributes and methods of the extended class, as in the following example:

```
class Client extends Person {
  address: string;
  constructor(name: string, age: number, address: string) {
    super(name, age);
    this.address = address;
  }
  toString(): string {
    return `${super.toString()} Address: ${this.address}`;
  }
}
```

Here, we are creating the `Client` class, which extends from the `Person` class. We add an attribute called `address` and create the constructor. As it is a class derived from `Person`, it is necessary to call the `super` method, which is the way we access the methods and attributes of the original class.

When using inheritance, we can optionally rewrite a method of the original class as we do with the `toString` method. This concept exists in JavaScript, but with TypeScript, the rules for the constructor and method rewrite are checked at compile time, giving us more confidence in our development.

Interfaces

In TypeScript, we have another way of typifying the structure of an object called an **interface**. The following example demonstrates its use:

```
export interface Animal {
  species: string;
  kingdom: string;
  class: string;
}
```

To declare an interface, we use the reserved word `interface` and declare its properties as a class as we saw earlier.

To use `interface`, we can proceed as follows:

```
import { Animal } from "./animals";

export function basic_interface() {
  let chicken: Animal = {
    kingdom: "Animalia",
    species: "Gallus",
    class: "birds",
```

```
};

console.log(
    `kingdom:${chicken.kingdom} species:${chicken.species}
class:${chicken.class}`
  );
}
```

Note that to use a class, we just type the variable and declare its values, without using the reserved word new. This happens because the interface is not a JavaScript element and is only used by the TypeScript transpiler to check whether the object contains the defined properties.

To prove that the interface does not exist, if we transpile the interface file, a blank file will be generated by TypeScript!

We can also make use of interfaces to create contracts for classes, should a class require certain methods and attributes. Let's see the following example:

```
export interface Animal {
   species: string;
   kingdom: string;
   class: string;
}
export interface DoSound {
   doASound: () => string;
}
export class Duck implements DoSound {
   public doASound(){
     return 'quack';
   }
}
export class Dog implements DoSound {
   public doASound(){
     return 'bark';
   }
}
```

To define that a certain class follows the DoSound contract, we use the reserved word implements. TypeScript then requires that a method called doASound be defined and that this method returns a string.

This feature of the interface facilitates the use of a very important capability of the object-oriented language, which is **polymorphism**. Let's see the example:

```
export function animalDoSound() {
   let duck = new Duck();
   let dog = new Dog();

   makeSound(duck);
   makeSound(dog);
}

function makeSound(animal: DoSound) {
   console.log(`The animal make this sound:${animal.doASound()}`);
}
```

We create the `makeSound` function, which receives an animal that implements the `DoSound` contract. The function is not concerned with the type of animal or its attributes; it just needs to follow the `DoSound` interface contract, as it will invoke one of its methods.

Angular uses this characteristic of TypeScript interfaces a lot, as we can see in the declaration of a component:

```
export class SimulationComponent implements OnInit {
```

When we inform Angular that the component implements the `OnInit` interface, it will execute the `ngOnInit` method required at the beginning of the component's lifecycle (we will study this in more detail in *Chapter 4, Components and Pages*).

Type aliases

The last way to type a variable that we will see in this chapter is the simplest one, which is to create **type aliases**. Like interfaces, type aliases only exist in TypeScript, and we can use them as in the following example:

```
type Machine = {
   id: number;
   description: string;
   energyOutput: number;
};

export function basic_type() {
   let car: Machine = {
      id: 123,
      description: "Car",
      energyOutput: 1000,
```

```
  };

  console.log(
    `ID:${car.id} Description:${car.description} Energy Output:${car.
energyOutput} `
  );
}
```

In this code, we create the `Machine` type, describing the object we want to represent, and in the `basic_type` function, we instantiate a variable with that type.

Note that we use the attributes of this variable just like the previous examples. This demonstrates how much TypeScript maintains the flexibility of JavaScript while giving more possibilities to the developer.

A well-used feature of type aliases is the creation of a type from other types. One of the most common is the union of types, as we can see in the following code:

```
type ID = string | number;
type Machine = {
  id: ID;
  description: string;
  energyOutput: number;
};
```

Here, we are creating a type called `id`, which can be `string` or `number`. For this, we use the `|` symbol, which is the same as used in JavaScript to indicate the conditional *OR*.

This feature was important for the use of more advanced techniques, such as the `guard` type, which we will see in this chapter.

When to use classes, interfaces, or types

With all these ways of creating typed objects, you must be wondering in which situations we should use each one. Based on the characteristics of each form, we can categorize the use of each one:

- **Type alias**: The simplest form of creation, recommended for typing input parameters and function returns.

- **Interfaces**: Recommended for representing JSON data objects, where we won't have methods, just the data representation. An example is the return of an API that we will use in our Angular project. The interface can also be used to define class contracts using the `implements` keyword.

- **Classes**: The basis of object orientation, also present in JavaScript. We should use it whenever we need an object with methods and attributes. In Angular, all components and services are ultimately objects created from classes.

Remember that in TypeScript, it is possible to create an `alias` type that behaves as an interface, as well as indicate an interface as a parameter and return of a function, but the recommendations here advise you to use the best for each type of situation and also explain how they are normally used in Angular apps.

Now that we have a good understanding of the different ways of creating more complex variables as objects, let's get to know how to create functions and methods with TypeScript.

Creating methods and functions

One of the best ways used by TypeScript to improve the developer experience in Angular application development is through the ability to type parameters and return functions and methods.

Both for developers who create libraries and frameworks and for those who consume these software components, knowing what a function expects and what the expected return is allows us to reduce the time spent reading and looking for documentation, especially the runtime bugs that our system may encounter.

To carry out the typing of the parameters and the return of a function, let's consider the following example:

```
interface invoiceItem {
  product: string;
  quantity: number;
  price: number;
}
type Invoice = Array<invoiceItem>;
function getTotalInvoice(invoice: Invoice): number {
  let invoiceTotal = invoice.reduce(
    (total, item) => total + item.quantity * item.price,
    0
  );
  return invoiceTotal;
}
export function invoiceExample() {
  let example: Invoice = [
    { product: "banana", price: 1.5, quantity: 3 },
    { product: "apple", price: 0.5, quantity: 5 },
    { product: "pinaple", price: 3, quantity: 12 },
  ];
  console.log(`Invoice Total:${getTotalInvoice(example)}`);
}
```

In this example, we start by defining an interface that represents an invoice item and then we create a type that will represent an invoice, which in this simplification is an array of items.

This demonstrates how we can use interfaces and types to better express our TypeScript code. Soon after, we create a function that returns the total value of the invoice; as an input parameter, we receive a value with the invoice type, and the return of the function will be a `number`.

Finally, we create an example function to use the `getTotalInvoice` function. Here, in addition to type checking, if we use an editor with TypeScript support such as VS Code, we have basic documentation and autocomplete, as shown in the following screenshot:

```
export function invoiceExample() {
  let example: Invoice = [
    { product: "banana", price: 1.5, quantity: 3 },
    { product: "apple", price: 0.5, quantity: 5 },
    { product: "pinaple", price: 3, quantity: 12 },
  ];
                          function getTotalInvoice(invoice: Invoice): number
  console.log(`Invoice Total:${getTotalInvoice(example)}`);
}
```

Figure 3.2 – Documentation generated by TypeScript and visualized by VS Code

In addition to primitive types and objects, functions must also be prepared to handle null data or undefined variables. In the next section, we will explore how to implement this.

Working with null values

In TypeScript, by default, all function and method parameters are required and checked by the transpiler.

If any parameter is optional, we can define it in the type it represents, as in the following example:

```
function applyDiscount(
  invoice: Invoice,
  discountValue: number,
  productOfDiscount?: string
) {
  discountValue = discountValue / 100;

  let newInvoice = invoice.map((item) => {
    if (productOfDiscount === undefined || item.product ===
productOfDiscount) {
      item.price = item.price - item.price * discountValue;
    }
    return item;
  });

  return newInvoice;
}
```

Within this function of applying a discount to the invoice, we created an optional parameter that allows the user of the function to determine a product to apply the discount. If the parameter is not defined, the discount is applied to the entire invoice.

To define an optional parameter, we use the ? character. In TypeScript, optional parameters must be the last to be defined in a function. If we change the position of the function parameters the following error is thrown by the transpiler:

```
error TS1016: A required parameter cannot follow an optional
parameter.
```

Additionally, TypeScript allows you to define a default value for the parameter:

```
function applyDiscount(
   invoice: Invoice,
   discountValue = 10,
   productOfDiscount?: string
)
```

When assigning a value in the parameter declaration, if the function user does not use the parameter, a 10% discount will be applied to the invoice items.

We've seen how we can use TypeScript to typify function parameters and returns. Now let's discuss type inference and how we can use it to reduce the verbosity of our code.

Decreasing verbosity – type inference

In this chapter, we saw the best TypeScript capabilities that help in the development of our Angular projects. We were typing all the variables and relying on the TypeScript transpiler to avoid errors that would otherwise occur in our user's runtime.

Let's now explore TypeScript's powerful inference mechanisms. Through it, TypeScript identifies the types of variables by content, not requiring you to define the type explicitly. Let's observe the following example:

```
export function primitive_example() {
   let name = "Mario";
   let age = 9;
   let isAlive = true;

   console.log(`Name:${name} Age:${age} is alive:${isAlive ? "yes" :
"no"}`);
}
```

This example is the same as in *Primitive and basic types*, but we directly inform the values in the variables. This way of declaring the variable has the same effect as the explicit method. If you change the value of a variable to another type, TypeScript will perform the validation as in the following example:

```
TSError: × Unable to compile TypeScript:
src/basic_types/primitive.ts:6:3 - error TS2322: Type 'number' is not
assignable to type 'string'.
```

TypeScript can also infer complex types, such as arrays and function returns. A good practice here is to use the inference capability to write less code and type only objects from interfaces, for example.

Validating types – type guards

Now that we know the TypeScript inference mechanism, we can understand another feature present in it, **type guards**. Let's consider these in the following example:

```
function getDiscount(value: string | number) {
  if (typeof value === "number") {
    return value;
  } else {
    return parseInt(value);
  }
}
```

In this function, we can receive a value that can be of the primitive types `string` or `number`.

As they are primitive types, we can use the `typeof` function to define whether the variable is numeric; otherwise, it is a string and we must convert it to numeric.

The TypeScript transpiler can interpret the context of this conditional and within each one, it treats the value as a `number` or `string`, including in VS Code's autocomplete.

Figure 3.3 – Inside the conditional TypeScript, which recognizes the variable as a number

The VS Code plugin in the figure is running the transpiler in the background and identifies that the variable inside the `if` statement can only be a `number`.

```
function getDiscount(value: string | number) {
    if (typeof value === "number") {
        return value;
    } else {                    (parameter) value: string
        return parseInt(value);
    }
}
    You, 5 minutes ago · Uncommitted changes
```

Figure 3.4 – Inside the conditional else TypeScript, which recognizes the variable as a string

As they are primitive types, we can use the typeof function to define whether the variable is numeric; otherwise, it is a string, and we must convert it to numeric.

For more complex data types such as objects, this guard using the typeof function is not possible because it will always recognize the variable of the object type. However, we can create our own custom type guard functions:

```
interface Person {
  socialSecurityNumber: number;
  name: string;
}

interface Company {
  corporateNumber: number;
  name: string;
}

type Client = Person | Company;

function isPerson(client: Client): client is Person {
  return (client as Person).socialSecurityNumber !== undefined;
}

function getID(client: Client) {
  if (isPerson(client)) {
    return client.socialSecurityNumber;
  } else {
    return client.corporateNumber;
  }
}
```

Here we have two interfaces, `Person` and `Company`, and we create a type called `Client`. For each type of object that follows the interfaces, we have an id type `socialSecurityNumber` for people and `corporateNumber` for companies.

To carry out the guard type, we created the `isPerson` function. The difference regarding this function is that we put the `client is Person` expression in the definition of the return of the function.

In it, we define the rule to consider an object as a person and use it in the `getID` function. Not only do we have a function that checks the object at runtime, but in this way, the TypeScript transpiler checks at compile time whether the operation has reported an error.

Using a better alternative to the any type

In the development of TypeScript applications, we may have situations where we do not know which type of parameter we are going to receive, such as the return of an API.

What is trafficked can be defined by creating an interface that represents the data, (for more details, see *Chapter 5, Angular Services and the Singleton Pattern*). It is not possible to guarantee this because pure text is trafficked on the internet.

In these cases, we can use the any type, which prevents TypeScript from doing the type checking.

In this example, we can see the use of any:

```
interface Products {
  id: number;
   description: string;
}

type ListOfProducts = Array<Products>;

const exampleList: ListOfProducts = [
  { id: 1, description: "banana" },
  { id: 2, description: "apple" },
  { id: 3, description: "pear" },
];

function getProductById(id: any) {
  return exampleList.find((product) => product.id === id);
}
```

In the preceding code sample, we create an interface that represents a product and a type that represents a list of products. We then create a function that receives an `id` of the any type and searches the `Array`, returning an item from the list of products.

In these simple examples, we can assume that there is no bug, but let's create a function that will use this snippet and see what happens:

```
export function getProductTest() {
  const id = '2';
  const item = getProductById(id);
  if (item !== undefined) {
    console.log(`ID:${item.id} Description:${item.description}`);
  } else {
    console.log("No product found");
  }
}
```

In this example, the item was not found because the variable we passed was a `string`. This could happen if the data we are passing to the function came from an API or external call, and the data was not properly formatted.

Running the code, we get the following result:

Figure 3.5 – Function returned No product found due to the id variable typing

When we use the `any` type, we give up the advantage of type checking and this type of bug can occur in our application. But how can we have the flexibility of the `any` type without losing TypeScript's type checking?

In these cases, we use the `unknown` type. This type has the same flexibility as the `any` type, but with one detail: TypeScript forces you to perform type guarding before using the variable.

Let's refactor our example function:

```
function getProductById(id: unknown) {
  if (typeof id === 'string'){
    id = parseInt(id);
  } else if (typeof id !== 'number'){
    return
  }

  return exampleList.find((product) => product.id === id);
}
```

Here we declare that `id` will be of an `unknown` type and, right after that, we make a `guard` type in this variable, dealing with the possible scenario of the variable being numerical.

The any type will still be used in your application, but consider using the unknown type to ensure correct type handling when you are not sure who will call your function.

Summary

In this chapter, we saw how we can use TypeScript to create better-quality code with less effort, increasing our productivity. We learned about basic TypeScript types, such as number, string, and Array.

We also studied creating classes, interfaces, and type aliases, and how we can choose and mix these types of structures to make our code cleaner and more maintainable.

Finally, we learned about TypeScript's type inference mechanism and how we can use the concept of type guards to further improve the type-checking mechanism. With these concepts, we also became familiar with the unknown type, which provides a better alternative to the any type.

In the next chapter we will learn about the basics of the interfaces of an Angular project, that is, the Components.

4

Components and Pages

The main building blocks of an Angular application are the **components**. It is by using them that we assemble our user interfaces and define the flow of the experience. In Angular architecture, components organize an application into reusable parts, making it easy to maintain and scale.

In this chapter, we will explore the communication between components and thus assemble our pages using component composition, avoiding the anti-pattern of creating monolithic interfaces.

In this chapter, we're going to cover the following topics:

- Creating components
- Communication between components – inputs and outputs
- Best practice – using the `TrackBy` property
- Separating responsibilities – smart and presentation components
- Communication from the child component – using `@Output`

By the end of this chapter, you will be able to create reusable and easy-to-maintain components and pages, streamlining the development of your project and increasing your productivity and that of your team.

Technical requirements

To follow the instructions in this chapter, you'll need the following:

- Visual Studio Code (`https://code.visualstudio.com/Download`)
- Node.js 18 or higher (`https://nodejs.org/en/download/`)

The code files for this chapter are available at `https://github.com/PacktPublishing/Angular-Design-Patterns-and-Best-Practices/tree/main/ch4`.

Creating components

Every interface created with Angular is a component in the architecture of the framework; therefore, theoretically, we could have our entire application in a single component.

As we studied in *Chapter 2, Organizing Your Application*, it is best to separate your application into modules, and with components, we use the same reasoning by separating our interfaces into and composing them with different components, maximizing reuse and maintainability.

In this chapter, we will illustrate this with a gym diary application, as shown in the following figure – to focus on Angular, we will not use Angular Material, only HTML, CSS (in this case, Tailwind CSS), and TypeScript.

Figure 4.1 – Gym diary application UI

In this initial example, we created a component with just the HTML template and the CSS and TypeScript files are as they were created by Angular CLI. Here's the top of the page first:

```
<div class="min-h-screen bg-gray-200">
  <header class="bg-blue-500 py-4 text-white">
    <div class="mx-auto max-w-6xl px-4">
      <h1 class="text-2xl font-bold">Workout diary</h1>
    </div>
  </header>
```

Using good HTML semantic practices, let's create a `main` section:

```
<main class="mx-auto mt-8 max-w-6xl px-4">
  <section class="mb-8">
    <h2 class="mb-4 text-xl font-bold">List of entries</h2>
```

```
    <ul class="rounded border shadow">
      <li class="mb-4 border-b bg-white p-4">
        <span class="font-bold">Date:</span> 2023-03-20<br />
        <span class="font-bold">Exercise:</span> Bench press<br />
        <span class="font-bold">Sets:</span> 3<br />
        <span class="font-bold">Reps:</span> 10
      </li>
        <!-- more entries here -->
    </ul>
  </section>
  <button
    class="rounded bg-blue-500 py-2 px-4 font-bold text-white
hover:bg-blue-700"
  >
    Add new entry
  </button>
</main>
</div>
```

We can see that in the preceding example, the interface is designed and stylized, but it is not functional because the diary entries are fixed in HTML, and in our application, the user should be able to add as many entries as they want.

We can identify here that this part of the diary entry could be a component for the page to use, so let's create a component called `entry`. As we learned in *Chapter 1, Starting Projects the Right Way*, we are going to use the Angular CLI to create this new component in the module we need:

```
ng g c diary/entry-item
```

With this command, the Angular CLI will create a folder with the following four files in addition to updating the `diary` module with the new component.

- `entry-item.component.css`: This file will contain the component's style sheet. Angular manages to solve a big pain point of a web application, which is the CSS scope of each component. With this feature, we can specify the component's styling without having to worry about whether it will affect an application's CSS even using the same property or selector name.

- `entry-item.component.html`: This file contains the component's HTML template and, although the extension seems to indicate that we can only use HTML tags, in the template file, we can use Angular directives, as we will study in this chapter.

- `entry-item.component.spec.ts`: This file contains the unit test for the component, which we will detail in *Chapter 10, Design for Tests: Best Practices*.

- `entry-item.component.ts`: This is the TypeScript file that represents the component itself. All other files are optional, making it possible for you to create a component with just this file, although this is not a practice widely applied in Angular projects and is only recommended for very small components.

In the `entry-item.component.ts` file, the Angular CLI created the following structure:

```
import { Component } from '@angular/core';

@Component({
  selector: 'app-entry-item',
  templateUrl: './entry-item.component.html',
  styleUrls: ['./entry-item.component.css']
})
export class EntryItemComponent {
}
```

With this example, we reinforce the definition that a component is a TypeScript class, and by using the `@Component` decorator, we indicate to Angular where the parts to assemble it are.

The main properties are as follows:

- `selector`: This is an optional property that defines what the component's selector will be if it is used in the template of another component. Components that represent a page do not need to have a selector defined as they are instantiated from a route. The Angular CLI suggests the selector based on your application's prefix defined in the `prefix` property of the `angular.json` file, along with the name you defined in the `ng g` command.

- `templateUrl`: This defines the path of the HTML file that contains the component's template. Alternatively, we can use the `template` property to define a string with all the component's HTML.

- `styleUrls`: This defines the path of the CSS files that contain the component's styling. A detail of this property is that it is an array, so it is possible to have more than one CSS file linked to the component. Alternatively, we can use the `style` property to define a string containing the component's CSS.

In the `entry-item.component.html` file, we will place the snippet that represents an item in a list of exercises in our gym diary:

```
<div class="mb-4 border-b bg-white p-4">
  <span class="font-bold">Date:</span> 2023-03-20<br />
  <span class="font-bold">Exercise:</span> Bench press<br />
  <span class="font-bold">Sets:</span> 3<br />
  <span class="font-bold">Reps:</span> 10
</div>
```

Here, we have the representation of an item, with the difference being that we are using the `<div>` element instead of `<li>` because we want our component to be as reusable as possible here – it may not necessarily be used within a list and within an `<ul>` element.

Let's put our component to use. In the `diary.component` component, let's refactor the `diary.component.html` file as follows:

```
<div class="min-h-screen bg-gray-200">
  <header class="bg-blue-500 py-4 text-white">
    <div class="mx-auto max-w-6xl px-4">
      <h1 class="text-2xl font-bold">Workout diary</h1>
    </div>
  </header>
  <main class="mx-auto mt-8 max-w-6xl px-4">
    <section class="mb-8">
      <h2 class="mb-4 text-xl font-bold">List of entries</h2>
      <ul class="rounded border shadow">
        <li>
          <app-entry-item />
        </li>
        <li>
          <app-entry-item />
        </li>
        <!-- more entries here -->
      </ul>
    </section>
    <button
      class="rounded bg-blue-500 py-2 px-4 font-bold text-white
hover:bg-blue-700"
    >
      Add new entry
    </button>
  </main>
</div>
```

Using the `app-entry-item` selector, we are consuming our new component on the page. From version 15 of Angular, we can use self-closing tags for components, so we have used `<app-entry-item />` here, but if you prefer the previous way, `<app-entry-item> </app-entry- item>` also still works.

Running our project, we can see that it continues to work. However, the data is the same in both items. We now need a way to pass information between components, and we'll see how to do that in the next section.

Communication between components – inputs and outputs

In our gym diary application, we now need the workout list page component, `DiaryComponent`, to communicate with the list item component, `EntryItemComponent`.

The simplest way to accomplish this communication is with Angular's Property Binding concept. Despite the complicated name, in practice, we annotate a component object's property with the `@Input` annotation, so Angular creates a custom HTML attribute on the component.

Let's see this concept in practice; first, let's create an interface that will represent an item in our diary:

```
ng g interface diary/interfaces/exercise-set
```

With the preceding command, we create the file and, as an organized practice, we create a folder to store the module's interfaces. In the generated file, we will define the object we want to communicate with:

```
export interface ExerciseSet {
  id?: string;
  date: Date;
  exercise: string;
  sets: number;
  reps: number;
}
export type ExerciseSetList = Array<ExerciseSet>;
```

We create an interface defining the object and a type to define a list of exercises, improving the future readability of our implementation.

Now, in the `entry-item.component.ts` file, let's add the new property:

```
import { Component, Input } from '@angular/core';
import { ExerciseSet } from '../interfaces/exercise-set';

@Component({
  selector: 'app-entry-item',
  templateUrl: './entry-item.component.html',
  styleUrls: ['./entry-item.component.css']
})
export class EntryItemComponent {
  @Input('exercise-set') exerciseSet!:ExerciseSet;
}
```

Here we create a property called `exerciseSet` of type `ExerciseSet` that we just defined. We use the ! symbol in the type definition because we are going to define its value at runtime.

The @Input annotation receives the exercise-set string as a parameter. With this, we define the name of the custom HTML attribute to be used in the template. This parameter is optional; if it's not used, the name of the attribute will be the name of the property. Here, it would be exerciseSet.

Let's now change our template to use this property:

```
<div class="mb-4 border-b bg-white p-4">
  <span class="font-bold">Date:</span> {{ exerciseSet.date | date
}}<br />
  <span class="font-bold">Exercise:</span> {{ exerciseSet.exercise
}}<br />
  <span class="font-bold">Sets:</span> {{ exerciseSet.sets }}<br />
  <span class="font-bold">Reps:</span> {{ exerciseSet.reps }}
</div>
```

To use the component's properties inside the template, we use the {{ }} syntax. Here, we can see an advantage of using VS Code with the Angular Language Service extension enabled because we have type-checking in the HTML template, avoiding typos, for example.

Something to highlight in this example is the Date attribute. Here, we are using an Angular feature called pipe, which allows the formatting of a template element. In this case, we are formatting a date.

Let's now configure a list of exercises in the diary.component.ts file:

```
import { Component } from '@angular/core';
import { ExerciseSetList } from '../interfaces/exercise-set';

@Component({
  templateUrl: './diary.component.html',
  styleUrls: ['./diary.component.css'],
})
export class DiaryComponent {
  exerciseList: ExerciseSetList = [
    { id: '1', date: new Date(), exercise: 'Deadlift', reps: 15, sets:
3 },
    { id: '2', date: new Date(), exercise: 'Squat', reps: 15, sets: 3
},
    { id: '3', date: new Date(), exercise: 'Barbell row', reps: 15,
sets: 3 },
  ];
}
```

For this example, we create a property called exerciseListExample and fill it with objects from the ExerciseSet interface. Now, let's change the list template in the diary.component.html file:

```
. . .
  <section class="mb-8">
```

```
    <h2 class="mb-4 text-xl font-bold">List of entries</h2>
      <ul class="rounded border shadow">
        <li *ngFor="let item of exerciseList">
          <app-entry-item [exercise-set]="item" />
        </li>
      </ul>
    </section>
    . . .
```

In the template, we are using the ngFor directive, which has the function of iterating over a list and rendering the element we want to define in the template. For each list item, we are going to create a new app-entry-item component and now we want to assign an item to it.

To do that, we use the [exercise-set] attribute to pass the item provided by ngFor. When we run our project, we have the list, as shown in the following figure:

Figure 4.2 – Gym diary application UI after refactoring

With this, we understand how to pass information from one component to another, but we can improve this project by introducing a good performance practice, the TrackBy property.

Best practice – using the TrackBy property

After the *ngIf directive, the ngFor directive will probably be the directive that you will use the most in your Angular projects. Although simple, this directive can hide a performance and perception problem in the frontend that will occur for your user.

To demonstrate this, let's add a new list button, simulating a list update coming from the backend.

In the diary.component.ts file, add the following method:

```
newList() {
  this.exerciseList = [
    { id: '1', date: new Date(), exercise: 'Deadlift', reps: 15,
sets: 3 },
    { id: '2', date: new Date(), exercise: 'Squat', reps: 15, sets: 3
},
    { id: '3', date: new Date(), exercise: 'Barbell row', reps: 15,
sets: 3 },
    { id: '4', date: new Date(), exercise: 'Leg Press', reps: 15,
sets: 3 },
  ];
}
```

This method replaces the array with this new array, which contains the same elements but with one more item.

Let's add the button to the list template:

```
<br>
<br>
  <button
    class="rounded bg-blue-500 py-2 px-4 font-bold text-white
hover:bg-blue-700"
    (click)="newList()"
  >
    Server Sync
  </button>
```

When we click on the **Server Sync** button, the entire item list is rendered, even though the new list is identical to the original except for the addition of a new item.

Figure 4.3 – Chrome DevTools

For a few items, this may not necessarily be a problem, but for a larger list, this unnecessary rendering may offend the performance perception our user will have of our application.

To improve this kind of case, the `ngFor` directive has the `TrackBy` option. Let's refactor our code to demonstrate this option; first, let's create a method for the exercise list component:

```
itemTrackBy(index: number, item: ExerciseSet) {
  return item.id;
}
```

This method tells Angular how to identify the single element in a collection that it will iterate through the `*ngFor` directive. Think of it as the *primary key* of the collection.

In the component's template, let's change the `ngFor` configuration:

```
<section class="mb-8">
  <h2 class="mb-4 text-xl font-bold">List of entries</h2>
  <ul class="rounded border shadow">
    <li *ngFor="let item of exerciseList; index as i; trackBy:
itemTrackBy">
      <app-entry-item [exercise-set]="item" />
    </li>
  </ul>
</section>
```

Here, we are telling `ngFor` to render based on the `id` property of the object. Running it again in the browser with Chrome DevTools, we see that now only the item with the `id` attribute is rendered on the page.

The `TrackBy` attribute, in addition to avoiding unnecessary rendering, has the following advantages:

- Enables animations when removing and adding items from the collection
- Retains any DOM-specific UI state, such as focus and text selection, when the collection changes

Now that we've learned about the use of this `ngFor` property, let's study how we can architect the composition of our components and pages.

Separating responsibilities – Smart and Presentation components

The information flow of a **single-page application (SPA)** can be quite complex and, if you don't think about this flow from the beginning of your design, it can affect the productivity and quality of your project over time.

The simpler the better; therefore, a very common design pattern not only in Angular applications but also in SPAs in general is the composition of interfaces using Smart and Presentation components. In literature and in the community, you will also find this pattern under the name of **Smart** and **Dumb** components or **Container** and **Presentation** components.

A Smart component has the UI business rule; it is where we will have injected the services that will communicate with the backend and where the interface with the Presentation components will be composed.

A Presentation component is a component that has the sole purpose of showing the data passed by the Smart component, normally via input. A Presentation component in turn can contain one or more components of the Presentation type.

To illustrate this pattern, we will use the following diagram:

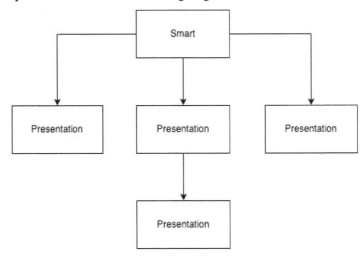

Figure 4.4 – Smart and Presentation components

Notice that we have a source of truth, which is the Smart component, and the communication occurs in only one direction, this is what we call a Unidirectional Data Flow. The purpose of this pattern is to isolate all states within a component and thereby simplify state management.

Let's refactor our project to fit this design pattern. Let's create a new presentation component using the Angular CLI:

```
ng g c diary/list-entries
```

In this new component, we are going to move the part that renders the list of diary entries into your template. In the list-entries.component.html file, add the following code:

```
<section class="mb-8">
  <h2 class="mb-4 text-xl font-bold">List of entries</h2>
  <ul class="rounded border shadow">
    <li *ngFor="let item of exerciseList; index as i; trackBy:
itemTrackBy">
      <app-entry-item [exercise-set]="item" />
    </li>
  </ul>
</section>
```

The list that will be displayed will come ready from the `DiaryComponent` component, so in the `list-entries.component.ts` file, we will add the following code:

```
import { Component, Input } from '@angular/core';
import { ExerciseSet, ExerciseSetList } from '../interfaces/exercise-
set';

@Component({
  selector: 'app-list-entries',
  templateUrl: './list-entries.component.html',
  styleUrls: ['./list-entries.component.css'],
})
export class ListEntriesComponent {
  @Input() exerciseList!: ExerciseSetList;

  itemTrackBy(index: number, item: ExerciseSet) {
    return item.id;
  }
}
```

Here, we move the `itemTrackBy` function into the component, as it will be its function to display the list, and we include the `exerciseList` attribute with the `@Input` decorator. In this example, we didn't specify any parameters, so the name of the template's attribute will be the same as the attribute of the `exerciseList` class.

Let's change the `Diary` template in the `diary.component.html` file to use the new presentation component we have created:

```
<main class="mx-auto mt-8 max-w-6xl px-4">
  <app-list-entries [exerciseList]="exerciseList" />
  <button
    class="rounded bg-blue-500 py-2 px-4 font-bold text-white
hover:bg-blue-700"
  >
    Add new entry
  </button>
  <br />
  <br />
  <button
    class="rounded bg-blue-500 py-2 px-4 font-bold text-white
hover:bg-blue-700"
    (click)="newList()"
  >
    erver Sync
  </button>
</main>
```

The `DiaryComponent` Smart component just passes the list to the `ListEntriesComponent` Presentation component, which iterates over the list by calling the `EntryItemComponent` Presentation component. With this structure, only the `DiaryComponent` component needs to worry about the list of exercises, respecting SOLID's Single Responsibility concept.

We've studied how to structure our pages and components, but how do child components communicate with their parents? Let's learn about the output attributes of Angular components next.

Communication from the child component – using @Output

We studied how parent components, which can be either smart or presentational, can communicate with their child components by using attributes marked with the `@Input` decorator.

However, when we need the opposite, the child component passes some information to the parent. As we saw in the previous section, business rule processing should ideally happen in the Smart component. For this type of communication, we mark attributes with the `@Output` decorator.

Let's create a button for adding an item to our diary. We'll see the use of forms in *Chapter 6, Handling User Input: Forms*, but here we want to focus on the interaction between components.

Using the Angular CLI, we will create the new component using this command:

```
ng g c diary/new-item-button
```

In the new component's template, let's move the diary button template into the component:

```
<button
  class="rounded bg-blue-500 py-2 px-4 font-bold text-white hover:bg-
blue-700"
>
  Add new entry
</button>
```

In the `new-item-button.component.ts` file, we will add the new attribute:

```
import { Component, EventEmitter, Output } from '@angular/core';
import { ExerciseSet } from '../interfaces/exercise-set';

@Component({
  selector: 'app-new-item-button',
  templateUrl: './new-item-button.component.html',
  styleUrls: ['./new-item-button.component.css'],
})
export class NewItemButtonComponent {
```

```
@Output() newExerciseEvent = new EventEmitter<ExerciseSet>();

addNewExercise() {
  const id = Date.now().toString();
  const date = new Date();
  const reps = 10;
  const sets = 4;
  const exercise = 'Leg Press';

  const newExerciseSet: ExerciseSet = { id, date, reps, sets,
exercise };
  this.newExerciseEvent.emit(newExerciseSet);
  }
}
```

Here, we first create the newExerciseEvent attribute and add the @Output decorator to define that it will be an attribute present in the component's template.

Here, there is a difference from the @Input attribute; in this case, we are already assigning an object of the EventEmitter class to the variable. This Angular class aims to emit events when a certain action takes place.

This is necessary because, unlike @Input, the value of which is assigned when the component is structured and rendered, @Output communication can occur at any time, depending on the user's action.

The EventEmitter class uses TypeScript's type-checking capability, making it possible for us to determine what type of object we are going to emit to the parent component.

In the addNewExercise method, we create an object of type ExerciseSet, and using the emit method of the EventEmitter class, we pass this object to the parent component.

Back to the template – let's add the method call to the button's click action:

```
<button
  class="rounded bg-blue-500 py-2 px-4 font-bold text-white hover:bg-
blue-700"
  (click)="addNewExercise()"
>
  Add new entry
</button>
```

Now let's refactor DiaryComponent to consume the new button:

```
. . .
<main class="mx-auto mt-8 max-w-6xl px-4">
  <app-list-entries [exerciseList]="exerciseList" />
```

```
    <app-new-item-button (newExerciseEvent)="addExercise($event)" />
    <br />
    <br />
    <button
      class="rounded bg-blue-500 py-2 px-4 font-bold text-white
hover:bg-blue-700"
      (click)="newList()"
    >
      Server Sync
    </button>
  </main>
  . . .
```

In the template, we are using the `app-new-item-button` component to pass the `addExercise` function to the `newExerciseEvent` attribute.

Here, we can highlight that the binding of an `@Output` attribute must be done with parentheses – `( )` – and this `$event` parameter represents the object that the child component will emit. If you highlight this parameter in VS Code, we can verify that it is of type `ExerciseSet`.

Finally, let's create the `addExercise` method in the component:

```
  . . .
  addExercise(newSet: ExerciseSet) {
      this.exerciseList.push(newSet);
  }
  . . .
```

Our method receives the emitted value and adds it to the `exercises` array. Running our project, we can see that the items are successfully added.

In this example, we can see in practice the whole flow of the design pattern of the Smart and presentation components. When clicking on the **Add Exercises** button, the `Diary` Smart component receives the new exercise from the `NewItemButtonComponent` presentation component.

By updating the list, the list is automatically passed to the `ListEntriesComponent` component, which renders the list on the screen. Now we are going to implement actions for the items of the list of exercises – we will see how to emit events of these items and how to identify these elements.

Propagating events from nested components

We will add the options to delete an item from the list and increase the number of repetitions to our diary. First, let's add the buttons to the list item template. In the `entry-item.component.html` file, we will edit the template:

```
<div class="mb-4 flex items-center justify-between border-b bg-white
p-4">
  <div>
    <span class="font-bold">Date:</span> {{ exerciseSet.date | date
}}<br />
    <span class="font-bold">Exercise:</span> {{ exerciseSet.exercise
}}<br />
    <span class="font-bold">Sets:</span> {{ exerciseSet.sets }}<br />
    <span class="font-bold">Reps:</span> {{ exerciseSet.reps }}
  </div>
  <div class="flex items-center">
    <button
      class="mr-2 rounded bg-red-500 py-2 px-4 font-bold text-white
hover:bg-red-700"
    >
      Delete
    </button>
    <button
      class="rounded bg-blue-500 py-2 px-4 font-bold text-white
hover:bg-blue-700"
    >
      New Rep
    </button>
  </div>
</div>
```

The challenge here is to ensure that the action that will happen on each item in the list if correctly identified to be applied correctly – that is, the Diary Smart component that handles the list will find the corresponding item and change it.

For this, we will apply the Angular output feature to the item component:

```
@Output() newRepEvent = new EventEmitter<ExerciseSet>();
@Output() deleteEvent = new EventEmitter<string>();

delete() {
  this.deleteEvent.emit(this.exerciseSet.id);
}

newRep() {
  const reps = ++this.exerciseSet.reps;
  const newItem: ExerciseSet = {
    ...this.exerciseSet,
    reps,
  };
```

```
        this.newRepEvent.emit(newItem);
    }
```

We create two outputs, each one for a different event that we want to emit, and we type them because we need different actions.

We then create the `delete` method, which will emit the `id` value of the item we want to delete, and the `newRep` method, with which we will add repetitions to the item of the exercise that will be performed and emit that item.

We will return to the template to associate the methods with the buttons created:

```
    <button
        class="mr-2 rounded bg-red-500 py-2 px-4 font-bold text-white
    hover:bg-red-700"
        (click)="delete()"
    >
        Delete
    </button>
    <button
        class="rounded bg-blue-500 py-2 px-4 font-bold text-white
    hover:bg-blue-700"
        (click)="newRep()"
    >
        New Rep
    </button>
```

Now let's change the `list-entries.component` presentation component for creating the output, which here, for simplicity, will have the same name as the item's output:

```
export class ListEntriesComponent {
    @Input() exerciseList!: ExerciseSetList;
    @Output() newRepEvent = new EventEmitter<ExerciseSet>();
    @Output() deleteEvent = new EventEmitter<string>();


    . . .

}
```

To propagate the item's events, we will change the list template:

```
    <li *ngFor="let item of exerciseList; index as i; trackBy:
    itemTrackBy">
        <app-entry-item
            [exercise-set]="item"
            (deleteEvent)="deleteEvent.emit($event)"
            (newRepEvent)="newRepEvent.emit($event)"
```

```
        />
    </li>
```

We can see that we only emit the item's event using the `emit` method of the outputs.

Finally, we will refactor the `DiaryComponent` Smart component to react to the item's event. First, let's see the template:

```
<main class="mx-auto mt-8 max-w-6xl px-4">
    <app-list-entries
        [exerciseList]="exerciseList"
        (deleteEvent)="deleteItem($event)"
        (newRepEvent)="newRep($event)"
    />
    . . .
</main>
```

As in the previous example, we used parentheses to associate it with a method, which will handle the event and receive the element emitted by the parameter of that method using the `$event` variable.

We will now refactor the component by creating two new methods – one to delete a journal entry and one to create a new repetition for an exercise:

```
. . .
deleteItem(id: string) {
    this.exerciseList = this.exerciseList.filter((item) => item.id !==
id);
}

  newRep(exerciseSet: ExerciseSet) {
    const id = exerciseSet.id;
    const i = this.exerciseList.findIndex((item) => item.id === id);
    if (i >= 0) {
      this.exerciseList[i] = { ...exerciseSet };
    }
  }
. . .
```

We are using the TypeScript array methods to simulate deleting and changing the array of items. We can see that the method already receives the deletion item or id automatically due to Angular's event emission mechanism.

We are taking advantage of the smart and presentation component pattern here to leverage its usage with a slightly more complex requirement.

Summary

In this chapter, we studied the elements responsible for rendering the interface of our project, the components. We saw how to create and organize the components in a granular way, resulting in our project being more maintainable.

We also studied how to communicate between components using the `@Input` and `@Output` attributes, using the capabilities of Angular that facilitate this communication.

We saw the good practice of using `TrackBy` to iterate lists in templates using the `ngFor` directive, improving performance specifically for lists with many items.

Finally, we study the design pattern of the Smart and Presentation components, a way of organizing components and their interactions in order to simplify this orchestration with a unidirectional information flow.

In the next chapter, we will study the Angular elements responsible for the business rules and interaction with the backend – the services.

5

Angular Services and the Singleton Pattern

One of the great differences between a static web page and a single-page application is the processing capacity and interaction in the user's browser, giving the feeling of an application installed on the device. In the Angular framework, the elements for this processing and interaction, not only with the backend but with the user, are the **services**.

This element is so important to Angular that the team created a dependency management system, which allows a simplified way of creating, composing, and using services in components.

In this chapter, we will explore this element and learn about the design patterns it uses and the best practices to use in your project.

Here we will cover the following topics:

- Creating services
- Understanding the dependency injection pattern
- Communication between components using services
- REST API consumption

By the end of the chapter, you will be able to create reusable and maintainable services, in addition to understanding practices that will improve your productivity.

Technical requirements

To follow the instructions in this chapter, you'll need the following:

- Visual Studio Code (https://code.visualstudio.com/Download)
- Node.js 18 or higher (https://nodejs.org/en/download/)

The code files for this chapter are available at `https://github.com/PacktPublishing/Angular-Design-Patterns-and-Best-Practices/tree/main/ch5`.

Creating services

Services in Angular are TypeScript classes that aim to implement business logic for our interfaces. Business logic in a frontend project can seem like a controversial issue because ideally, all logic and processing should take place on the backend, which is correct.

Here we are using business rules; these rules are generic behaviors that do not depend on a visual component and can be reused in other components.

Examples of frontend business rules could be as follows:

- Application state control
- Communication with the backend
- Information validations with a fixed rule, such as the number of digits in a telephone number

We are going to put this concept into practice, and in our gym diary application, we are going to create the first service. In the command line we will use the Angular CLI:

```
ng generate service diary/services/ExerciseSets
```

Unlike the component, we can see that the element created by the Angular CLI is composed only of a TypeScript file (and its corresponding unit test file).

In this file, we will see the boilerplate that the Angular CLI generated:

```
import { Injectable } from '@angular/core';
@Injectable({
  providedIn: 'root'
})
export class ExerciseSetsService {
  constructor() { }
}
```

Here we have a TypeScript class called `ExerciseSetsService` with a decorator called `@Injectable`. It is this decorator that characterizes a service in Angular; we will see more details about it later in this chapter.

Let's refactor our project and place the initial series of sets for our diary in this service.

First, we'll create the methods that will get the initial list and refresh it in the backend:

```
private setList?: ExerciseSetList;

getInitialList(): ExerciseSetList {
  this.setList = [
    { id: 1, date: new Date(), exercise: 'Deadlift', reps: 15, sets: 3
},
    { id: 2, date: new Date(), exercise: 'Squat', reps: 15, sets: 3 },
    { id: 3, date: new Date(), exercise: 'Barbell row', reps: 15,
sets: 3 },
  ];
  return this.setList;
}


refreshList(): ExerciseSetList {
  this.setList = [
    { id: 1, date: new Date(), exercise: 'Deadlift', reps: 15, sets: 3
},
    { id: 2, date: new Date(), exercise: 'Squat', reps: 15, sets: 3 },
    { id: 3, date: new Date(), exercise: 'Barbell row', reps: 15,
sets: 3 },
    { id: 4, date: new Date(), exercise: 'Leg Press', reps: 15, sets:
3 },
  ];
  return this.setList;
}
```

In the service, we move the initialization and refresh of the journal component into the service, using the getInitialList and refreshList methods.

These methods will be improved when we see the communication with the backend, but here, we are already decoupling the exercise list management business rule from the component that renders the user interface, creating a specific service.

Let's now consider the method that adds an item to the exercise list:

```
addNewItem(item: ExerciseSet): ExerciseSetList {
  if (this.setList) {
    this.setList = [...this.setList, item];
  } else {
    this.setList = [item];
  }
  return this.setList;
}
```

The `setList` attribute of the service can be null, so here we use the TypeScript type guard concept (more details in *Chapter 3, TypeScript Patterns for Angular*) to manipulate the array. Here, we also use the concept of immutability by returning a new array after adding the new element.

In the `DiaryComponent` component, we will use the service we created:

```
export class DiaryComponent {
  constructor(private exerciseSetsService: ExerciseSetsService) {}
  exerciseList = this.exerciseSetsService.getInitialList();
  newList() {
    this.exerciseList = this.exerciseSetsService.refreshList();
  }
  addExercise(newSet: ExerciseSet) {
    this.exerciseList = this.exerciseSetsService.addNewItem(newSet);
  }
}
```

In the component, the first thing we can observe is the use of the class constructor, declaring an `exerciseSetsService` private attribute of type `ExerciseSetsService`. With this declaration, we have an object instantiated and we refactor our component, replacing the initialization of the list and the refresh action with service methods.

From now on, it is no longer a concern of the component how the exercise list is obtained and managed; this is the responsibility of the service, and we can now use this service in other components if necessary. In this piece of code, you may be wondering why we are using the `ExerciseSetsService` service if we did not instantiate an object of that class.

Here, we have a great feature of Angular, which is the dependency injection mechanism, and we will delve into this topic next.

Understanding the dependency injection pattern

In object-oriented software development, it is good practice to prioritize composition over inheritance, meaning that a class should be composed of other classes (preferably interfaces).

In our previous example, we can see that the `service` class comprises the `DiaryComponent` component. Another way to use this service would be as follows:

```
. . .
export class DiaryComponent {
  private exerciseSetsService: ExerciseSetsService;
  exerciseList: ExerciseSetList;

  constructor() {
    this.exerciseSetsService = new ExerciseSetsService();
```

```
    this.exerciseList = this.exerciseSetsService.getInitialList();
  }
  . . .
}
```

Here we modify our code, leaving the creation of the service class object expressly in the component's constructor method. Running our code again, we can see that the interface remains the same.

This approach, although functional, has some problems, such as the following:

- High coupling between the component and the service, which means that we may encounter problems if we need to change the implementation of the service, for example, for the construction of unit tests

- If the service depends on another class, as we will see with Angular's HTTP request service, the HttpClient class, we will have to implement this dependency in our component, increasing its complexity

To simplify development and solve the problems we've described, Angular has a dependency injection mechanism. This feature allows us to compose a class just by declaring the object we need in its constructor.

Angular, leveraging TypeScript, will use the types defined in this declaration to assemble the dependency tree of the class we need and create the object we require.

Let's return to our code and analyze how this mechanism works:

```
  . . .
  export class DiaryComponent {
    constructor(private exerciseSetsService: ExerciseSetsService) {}

    exerciseList = this.exerciseSetsService.getInitialList();
  . . .
  }
```

In the code, we declare the dependency of our class in the constructor, creating the exerciseSetsService attribute. With this, we can initialize the exerciseList attribute in its declaration.

In *Chapter 10, Design for Tests: Best Practices*, we will replace the implementation of this service in the test runtime. All this is possible thanks to Angular's dependency injection feature.

From version 14 of Angular, we have an alternative for dependency injection that we can use, which we will see next.

Using the inject() function

The `inject()` function allows you to use the same dependency injection feature but in a simpler way.

Let's refactor our component's code:

```
import { Component, inject } from '@angular/core';
import { ExerciseSet } from '../interfaces/exercise-set';
import { ExerciseSetsService } from '../services/exercise-sets.
service';
. . .
export class DiaryComponent {
  private exerciseSetsService = inject(ExerciseSetsService);
  exerciseList = this.exerciseSetsService.getInitialList();
. . .
}
```

Here we remove the constructor declaration for the dependency injection and directly declare the `exerciseSetsService` service. For the creation of the object, we use the `inject` function.

A point of note is that we are using the `inject` function of the `@angular/core` module and not the function present in the `@angular/core/testing` module, which will be used for another purpose.

This method, in addition to being simpler and clearer (the service is being injected by the function), allows the simplification of development, if it is necessary to use inheritance for a specific component. Remembering that good practice says we should prefer composition over inheritance, but especially in libraries, this feature can be interesting.

A point of note for the use of the `inject` function is that it can only be used in the component's construction phase, that is, in the declaration of the method's property or in the class's constructor method.

Any use in another context will generate the following compilation error:

```
inject() must be called from an injection context
such as a constructor, a factory function, a field initializer,
or a function used with `runInInjectionContext`.
```

Let's now delve into another aspect of Angular services, which is the use of the singleton design pattern, and how we can use this capability for communication between components.

Communication between components using services

A characteristic that we must understand about Angular services is that, by default, every service instantiated by the dependency injection mechanism has the same reference; that is, a new object is not created, but reused.

This is because the dependency injection mechanism implements the singleton design pattern to create and deliver the objects. The **singleton pattern** is a design pattern of the creational type and allows the creation of objects whose access will be global in the system.

This characteristic is important for the service because, as the service deal with reusable business rules, we can use the same instance between components, without having to rebuild the entire object. In addition, we can take advantage of this characteristic and use services as an alternative for communication between components.

Let's change our gym diary so that the `ListEntriesComponent` component receives the initial list by service instead of `@Input`:

```
export class ListEntriesComponent {
  private exerciseSetsService = inject(ExerciseSetsService);
  exerciseList = this.exerciseSetsService.getInitialList();
  itemTrackBy(index: number, item: ExerciseSet) {
    return item.id;
  }
}
```

In the `DiaryComponent` component, we will remove the list from the input:

```
<main class="mx-auto mt-8 max-w-6xl px-4">
  <app-list-entries />
  <app-new-item-button (newExerciseEvent)="addExercise($event)" />
  <br />
  <br />
  <button
    class="rounded bg-blue-500 py-2 px-4 font-bold text-white
hover:bg-blue-700"
    (click)="newList()"
  >
    Server Sync
  </button>
</main>
```

Running it again we can see that the list continues to appear. This is because the instance of the service used in both components is the same. However, this form of communication requires us to use RxJS to update the values with the buttons on the diary screen. We will go deeper into this topic in *Chapter 9, Exploring Reactivity with RxJS*.

We saw that, by default, the services are singleton, but in Angular, it is possible to change this configuration for another service if you need to solve some corner cases in your application.

When we create a service, it has an @Injectable decorator, as in our example:

```
@Injectable({
  providedIn: 'root',
})
export class ExerciseSetsService {
```

The provideIn metadata determines the scope of the service. The value 'root' means that the instance of the service will be unique for every application; that's why, by default, Angular services are singleton.

To change this behavior, let's first return to the ListEntriesComponent component to receive @Input:

```
export class ListEntriesComponent {
  @Input() exerciseList!: ExerciseSetList;

  itemTrackBy(index: number, item: ExerciseSet) {
    return item.id;
  }
}
```

Let's go back to inform the attribute in the DiaryComponent component:

```
<main class="mx-auto mt-8 max-w-6xl px-4">
  <app-list-entries [exerciseList]="exerciseList" />
  <app-new-item-button (newExerciseEvent)="addExercise($event)" />
  <br />
  <br />
  <button
    class="rounded bg-blue-500 py-2 px-4 font-bold text-white
hover:bg-blue-700"
    (click)="newList()"
  >
    Server Sync
  </button>
</main>
```

In the ExerciseSetsService service, we will remove the provideIn metadata:

```
@Injectable()
export class ExerciseSetsService {
```

If we run our application now, the following error will occur:

```
ERROR Error: Uncaught (in promise): NullInjectorError:
R3InjectorError(DiaryModule)[ExerciseSetsService ->
ExerciseSetsService -> ExerciseSetsService -> ExerciseSetsService]:
NullInjectorError: No provider for ExerciseSetsService!
```

This error happens when we inform Angular that the service should not be instantiated in the application scope. To resolve this error, let's declare the use of the service directly in the `DiaryComponent` component:

```
@Component({
  templateUrl: './diary.component.html',
  styleUrls: ['./diary.component.css'],
  providers: [ExerciseSetsService],
})
export class DiaryComponent {
```

So, our system works again, and the component has its own instance of the service.

This technique, however, must be used in specific cases where the component must have its own instance of the services it uses; it is recommended to leave the `provideIn` in the services.

Let's now start exploring our application's communication with the backend using Angular.

REST API consumption

One of the main uses of Angular services is undoubtedly communication with the backend of the application, using the **Representational State Transfer** (**REST**) protocol.

Let's learn about this feature in practice by preparing our project to consume its backend.

First, let's upload the backend locally by accessing the `gym-diary-backend` folder and using the following command in your command-line prompt:

```
npm start
```

We can leave this command running and can now create the services for the consumption of the API.

To carry out this consumption, Angular has a specialized service – `HttpClient`. To use it, we will first import its module into the `app.module.ts` file:

```
import { NgModule } from '@angular/core';
import { BrowserModule } from '@angular/platform-browser';
import { AppRoutingModule } from './app-routing.module';
import { HttpClientModule } from '@angular/common/http';
```

```
import { AppComponent } from './app.component';

@NgModule({
  declarations: [AppComponent],
  imports: [BrowserModule, AppRoutingModule, HttpClientModule],
  providers: [],
  bootstrap: [AppComponent],
})
export class AppModule {}
```

Our project's backend API returns some JSON, containing the list of exercises for the day. As good practice, we should create an interface to facilitate typing and the manipulation of the results in our frontend application. In the exercise-set.ts file, we will add the following interface:

```
export interface ExerciseSetListAPI {
  hasNext: boolean;
  items: ExerciseSetList;
}
```

Now we can refactor our ExerciseSetsService service to use HttpClient:

```
export class ExerciseSetsService {
  private httpClient = inject(HttpClient);
  private url = 'http://localhost:3000/diary';
  getInitialList(): Observable<ExerciseSetListAPI> {
    return this.httpClient.get<ExerciseSetListAPI>(this.url);
  }
  refreshList(): Observable<ExerciseSetListAPI> {
    return this.httpClient.get<ExerciseSetListAPI>(this.url);
  }
}
```

First, we inject the HttpClient service into our class using the inject function. We then create the url variable to contain the endpoint of this service that will be used in the service's methods.

Finally, we refactor the getInitialList and refreshList methods to consume the project's API. Initially, they have the same implementation, but we will improve this code throughout the book.

An important change was made so that the method does not return the list of exercises, but an Observable that contains the list of exercises. This occurs because the operation involving consuming a REST API happens asynchronously, and through the use of RxJS and its Observables, Angular handles this asynchronicity. We will go deeper into this topic in *Chapter 9, Exploring Reactivity with RxJS*.

Using the `HttpClient` service to consume a *GET-type* API, we declare the return type represented here by the `ExerciseSetListAPI` type and the service's `get` method, passing the URL of the endpoint that we are going to consume as a parameter.

Let's now add the other methods to complete our service:

```
addNewItem(item: ExerciseSet): Observable<ExerciseSet> {
  return this.httpClient.post<ExerciseSet>(this.url, item);
}
updateItem(id: string, item: ExerciseSet): Observable<ExerciseSet> {
  return this.httpClient.put<ExerciseSet>(`${this.url}/${id}`, item);
  deleteItem(id: string): Observable<boolean> {
    return this.httpClient.delete<boolean>(`${this.url}/${id}`);
  }
}
```

For the inclusion of a new set, we are using the POST method of the service that calls the API with the verb of the same name. We always pass the URL and, in this case, the body of the request will be a new set of exercises.

To update the set, we use the PUT method passing the body, and for the URL, we use the string interpolation to pass the `id` value that the API demands in your contract. Finally, to delete, we use the DELETE method, and also using interpolation, we pass the `id` value of the element we want to delete.

Let's tailor our `DiaryComponent` component to consume the refactored service. Our challenge here is to deal with the asynchrony of consuming a REST API via an HTTP request.

First, let's adjust the initialization of the list of exercises:

```
@Component({
  templateUrl: './diary.component.html',
  styleUrls: ['./diary.component.css'],
})
export class DiaryComponent implements OnInit {
  private exerciseSetsService = inject(ExerciseSetsService);
  exerciseList!: ExerciseSetList;

  ngOnInit(): void {
    this.exerciseSetsService
      .getInitialList()
      .subscribe((dataApi) => (this.exerciseList = dataApi.items));
  }
}
```

In the `DiaryComponent` class, we will implement the `OnInit` interface and create the `onInit` method. This method is one of the lifecycle events of Angular components, which means that it will be called at some point by Angular when building and rendering the interface.

The `onInit` method is called after building the component, but before rendering the component. We need to implement this method because the filling of the list of exercises will occur asynchronously. Implementing this initialization in the `onInit` method will ensure that the data will be there when Angular starts rendering the screen.

In this method, we are using the service, but as it now returns an Observable, we need to call the `subscribe` method and, within it, implement the initialization of the list. As we are using the smart and presentation component architecture, we can implement the button methods in the `DiaryComponent` smart component as follows:

```
newList() {
  this.exerciseSetsService
    .refreshList()
    .subscribe((dataApi) => (this.exerciseList = dataApi.items));
}


addExercise(newSet: ExerciseSet) {
  this.exerciseSetsService
    .addNewItem(newSet)
    .subscribe((_) => this.newList());
}

deleteItem(id: string) {
  this.exerciseSetsService.deleteItem(id).subscribe(() => {
    this.exerciseList = this.exerciseList.filter(
      (exerciseSet) => exerciseSet.id !== id
    );
  });
}


newRep(updateSet: ExerciseSet) {
  const id = updateSet.id ?? '';
  this.exerciseSetsService
    .updateItem(id, updateSet)
    .subscribe();
}
```

In the `newList` method, we refactored this to fetch the list elements through the `refreshList` method.

In the `addExercise`, `deleteItem`, and `newRep` methods, we refactored the previous logic to use the `exerciseSetsService` service.

Summary

In this chapter, we learned about Angular services and how to correctly isolate the business rule from our applications in a simple and reusable way, as well as how Angular services use the singleton pattern for memory and performance optimization.

We worked with and studied Angular's dependency injection mechanism and noticed how important it is to be able to organize and reuse services between components and other services. We also learned how to use the `inject` function for Angular services as an alternative to dependency injection via Angular's constructor.

Finally, we worked with one of the main uses of services, communication with the backend, and in this chapter, we began to explore the integration of our frontend applications with the backend.

In the next chapter, we will study the best practices for using forms, the main way that our users enter information into our systems.

Part 2:
Leveraging Angular's Capabilities

In this part, you will work with more advanced aspects of Angular and see how you can use the features of this framework for the most common tasks in your applications. You will learn about best practices for forms, how to correctly use Angular's routing mechanism, and finally, how to optimize API consumption using the Interceptor design pattern and the RxJS library.

This part has the following chapters:

- *Chapter 6, Handling User Inputs: Forms*

- *Chapter 7, Routes and Routers*

- *Chapter 8, Improving Backend Integrations: the Interceptor Pattern*

- *Chapter 9, Exploring Reactivity with RXJS*

Handling User Inputs: Forms

Since the early days of web applications, before the concept of **Single Page Applications** (**SPAs**), in HTML 2, the <form> tag has been used to create, organize, and send forms to the backend.

In common applications, such as banking systems and health applications, we use forms to organize the inputs that our users need to perform in our systems. With such a common element in web applications, it is natural that Angular, a framework whose philosophy is *batteries included*, offers this feature to its developers.

In this chapter, we will delve into the following forms features in Angular:

- Template-driven forms
- Reactive forms
- Data validation
- Custom validations
- Typed reactive forms

By the end of this chapter, you will be able to create maintainable and fluid forms for your user, in addition to improving your productivity with this type of task.

Technical requirements

To follow the instructions in this chapter, you'll need the following:

- Visual Studio Code (https://code.visualstudio.com/Download)
- Node.js 18 or higher (https://nodejs.org/en/download/)

The code files for this chapter are available at https://github.com/PacktPublishing/Angular-Design-Patterns-and-Best-Practices/tree/main/ch6.

During the study of this chapter, remember to run the backend of the application found in the `gym-diary-backend` folder with the `npm start` command.

Template-driven forms

Angular has two different ways of working with forms: **template-driven** and **reactive**. First, let's explore template-driven forms. As we can see by the name, we maximize the use of the capabilities of the HTML template to create and manage the data model linked to the form.

We will evolve our Gym Diary application to better exemplify this concept. In the following command line, we use the Angular CLI to create the new page component:

```
ng g c diary/new-entry-form-template
```

To access the new assignment form, we'll refactor the journal page component so the **Add New Entry** button takes the user to the component we created.

Let's add to the `DiaryModule` module the import of the framework module responsible for managing the application's routes:

```
. . .
import { RouterModule } from '@angular/router';

@NgModule({
  declarations: [
    DiaryComponent,
    EntryItemComponent,
    ListEntriesComponent,
    NewItemButtonComponent,
    NewEntryFormTemplateComponent,
  ],
  imports: [CommonModule, DiaryRoutingModule, RouterModule],
})
export class DiaryModule {}
```

With the `RouterModule` module imported, we will be able to use Angular's route services. For more details on routing, see *Chapter 7, Routes and Routers*. We will add the new component to a route in the `DiaryRoutingModule` module:

```
. . .
import { NewEntryFormTemplateComponent } from './new-entry-form-
template/new-entry-form-template.component';

const routes: Routes = [
  {
```

```
    path: '',
    component: DiaryComponent,
  },
  {
    path: 'new-template',
    component: NewEntryFormTemplateComponent,
  },
];

@NgModule({
  imports: [RouterModule.forChild(routes)],
  exports: [RouterModule],
})
export class DiaryRoutingModule {}
```

To be able to compare the two form creation approaches, we will create a route for each example component that we are going to create. Here, the URL /home/new-template will direct us to the template-driven form route.

We will now refactor DiaryComponent to modify the behavior of the **Add New Entry** button:

```
. . .
import { Router } from '@angular/router';
@Component({
  templateUrl: './diary.component.html',
  styleUrls: ['./diary.component.css'],
})
export class DiaryComponent implements OnInit {
  private exerciseSetsService = inject(ExerciseSetsService);
  private router = inject(Router)
. . .
  addExercise(newSet: ExerciseSet) {
    this.router.navigate(['/home/new-template'])
  }
. . .
}
```

First, we need to inject Angular's router service.We change the addExercise method to use the service and, using the navigate method, direct to the page.

We can proceed to the HTML template of our form in the new-entry-form-template. component.html file and place only the elements of the form:

```
<div class="flex h-screen items-center justify-center bg-gray-200">
  <form class="mx-auto max-w-sm rounded bg-gray-200 p-4">
```

```
      . . .
      <input
        type="date"
        id="date"
         name="date"
    />
  . . .
      <input
        type="text"
        id="exercise"
        name="exercise"
      />
  . . .
      <input
        type="number"
        id="sets"
        name="sets"
      />
</div>
<input
  type="number"
  id="reps"
  name="reps"
/>
  </div>
  <div class="flex items-center justify-center">
    <button
      type="submit"
    >
    Add Entry
    </button>
...
```

Angular uses HTML best practices, so we will now create the form fields under the HTML `<form>` tag. In the input fields, we are respecting the HTML semantics and creating the fields as `<input>` with the correct types for the type of information the client needs.

Let's run our application with the `ng serve` command. By clicking on the **New Entry** button, we will be able to notice our diary entry addition form.

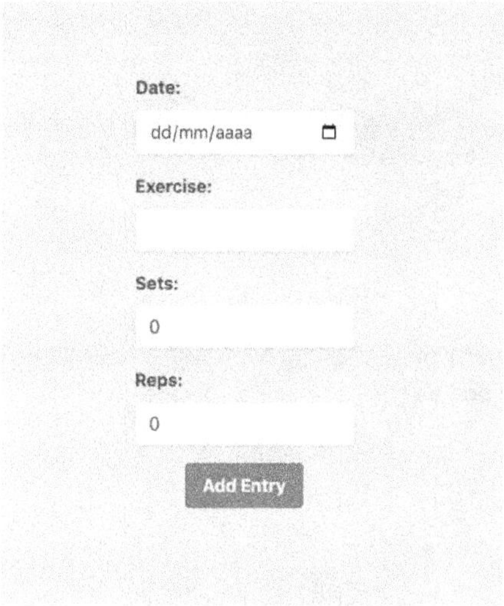

Figure 6.1 – Gym Diary Form UI

Here, we have the structure and template of our form. Now, we are going to prepare for Angular to manage the state of the fields via user input in the template. To use the template-driven form, we need to import the FormModule module to our feature module, DiaryModule:

```
import { FormsModule } from '@angular/forms';
@NgModule({
  declarations: [
    DiaryComponent,
    EntryItemComponent,
    ListEntriesComponent,
    NewItemButtonComponent,
    NewEntryFormTemplateComponent,
  ],
  imports: [CommonModule, DiaryRoutingModule, RouterModule,
FormsModule],
})
export class DiaryModule {}
```

In our form template, we will add the directives that will create and link the form information to its data model:

```
. . .
<form
  (ngSubmit)="newEntry()"
  class="mx-auto max-w-sm rounded bg-gray-200 p-4">
    <div class="mb-4">
```

```
    . . .
    <input type="date" id="date" name="date"
    . . .
    [(ngModel)]="entry.date"
/>
</div>
<div class="mb-4">
    . . .
    <input type="text" id="exercise" name="exercise"
[(ngModel)]="entry.exercise"
    . . . />
</div>
<div class="mb-4">
. . .
    <input type="number" id="sets" name="sets"  [(ngModel)]="entry.
sets"
. . ./>
</div>
<div class="mb-4">
. . .
    <input type="number" id="reps" name="reps" [(ngModel)]="entry.
reps"
. . ./>
. . .
</form>
</div>
{{ entry | json }}
```

The first change we need to make to our template is to use the ngSubmit parameter to state which method will be called by Angular when the user submits the form. Then, we link the HTML input elements with the data model that will represent the form. We do this through the [(ngModel)] directive.

ngModel is an object managed by the FormModule module that represents the form's data model. The use of square brackets and parentheses signals to Angular that we are performing a two-way data binding on the property.

This means that the ngModel property will both receive the form property and emit events. Finally, for development and debugging purposes, we are placing the content of the entry object in the footer and formatting it with the JSON pipe.

Let's finish the form by changing the component's TypeScript file:

```
export class NewEntryFormTemplateComponent {
private exerciseSetsService = inject(ExerciseSetsService);
private router = inject(Router);
```

```
entry: ExerciseSet = { date: new Date(), exercise: '', reps: 0, sets:
0 };
      newEntry() {
    const newEntry = { ...this.entry };
    this.exerciseSetsService
      .addNewItem(newEntry)
      .subscribe((entry) => this.router.navigate(['/home']));
  }
}
```

First, we inject the `ExerciseSetsService` service for the backend communication and the router service because we want to return to the diary as soon as the user creates a new entry.

Soon after we create the entry object that represents the form's data model, it is important that we start it with an empty object because Angular makes the binding as soon as the form is loaded. Finally, we create the `newEntry` method, which will send the form data to the backend through the `ExerciseSetsService` service.

For more details about Angular services, see *Chapter 5, Angular Services and the Singleton Pattern*. If we run our project and fill in the data, we can see that we are back to the diary screen with the new entry in it.

Notice that at no point did we need to interact with the entry object, as Angular's form template engine took care of that for us! This type of form can be used for simpler situations, but now we will see the way recommended by the Angular team to create all types of forms: reactive forms!

Reactive forms

Reactive forms use a declarative and explicit approach to creating and manipulating form data. Let's put this concept into practice by creating a new form for our project.

First, on the command line, let's use the Angular CLI to generate the new component:

```
ng g c diary/new-entry-form-reactive
```

In the same way as we did with the template-driven form, let's add this new component to the `DiaryRoutingModule` routing module:

```
import { NewEntryFormReactiveComponent } from './new-entry-form-
reactive/new-entry-form-reactive.component';

const routes: Routes = [
  {
    path: '',
    component: DiaryComponent,
  },
```

```
    {
      path: 'new-template',
      component: NewEntryFormTemplateComponent,
    },
    {
      path: 'new-reactive',
      component: NewEntryFormReactiveComponent,
    },
  ];
```

In the `DiaryModule` module, we need to add the `ReactiveFormsModule` module responsible for all the functionality that Angular makes available to us for this type of form:

```
@NgModule({
  declarations: [

    . . .

  ],
  imports: [

    . . .

    ReactiveFormsModule,
  ],
})
```

To finalize the component's route, let's change the main screen of our application, replacing the route that the **New Entry** button will call:

```
addExercise(newSet: ExerciseSet) {
  this.router.navigate(['/home/new-reactive']);
}
```

We will now start creating the reactive form. First, let's configure the component elements in the `new-entry-form-reactive.component.ts` TypeScript file:

```
export class NewEntryFormReactiveComponent implements OnInit {
  public entryForm!: FormGroup;
  private formBuilder = inject(FormBuilder);
  ngOnInit() {
    this.entryForm = this.formBuilder.group({
      date: [''],
      exercise: [''],
      sets: [''],
      reps: [''],
    });
  }
}
```

Note that the first attribute is entryForm of type FormGroup. It will represent our form—not just the data model, but the whole form—as validations, field structure, and so on.

Then, we inject the FormBuilder service responsible for assembling the entryForm object. Note the name of the service that Angular uses from the Builder design pattern, which has the objective of creating complex objects, such as a reactive form.

To initialize the entryForm attribute, we'll use the onInit component lifecycle hook. Here, we'll use the group method to define the form's data model. This method receives the object, and each attribute receives an array that contains the characteristics of that attribute in the form. The first element of the array is the initial value of the attribute.

In the component's template, we will create the structure of the form, which, in relation to the template-driven form example, is very similar:

```
<div class="flex h-screen items-center justify-center bg-gray-200">
  <form
    [formGroup]="entryForm"
  >
    <input
      type="date"
      id="date"
      name="date"
      formControlName="date"
    />
    <input
      type="text"
      id="exercise"
      name="exercise"
      formControlName="exercise"
    />
    <input
      type="number"
      id="sets"
      name="sets"
      formControlName="sets"
    />
    <input
      type="number"
      id="reps"
      name="reps"
      formControlName="reps"
    />
    <button type="submit">
      Add Entry
```

```
    </button>
{{ entryForm.value | json }}
```

The first difference is the use of the `formGroup` attribute to associate the template with the object we created earlier. To associate each template field to the `FormGroup` attribute, we use the `formControlName` element.

To debug the data model, we are also using the JSON pipe, but note that to get the data model filled in by the user, we use the `value` attribute of the `entryForm` object. Finally, we will complement the form with functionality and record the input using the project's API.

The next step is to change the component:

```
export class NewEntryFormReactiveComponent implements OnInit {
  . . .
  private exerciseSetsService = inject(ExerciseSetsService);
  private router = inject(Router);
  . . .
  newEntry() {
    const newEntry = { ...this.entryForm.value };
    this.exerciseSetsService
      .addNewItem(newEntry)
      .subscribe((entry) => this.router.navigate(['/home']));
  }
}
```

Here, we inject the consumer services of the `ExerciseSetsService` API and the Angular route service router.

In the `newEntry` method, as in the previous example, we capture the data that the user typed. However, in the reactive form, it is in the `value` attribute, and we send this attribute to the API using the service.

Running the project, we can see that the interface works like its counterpart written for the template-driven form.

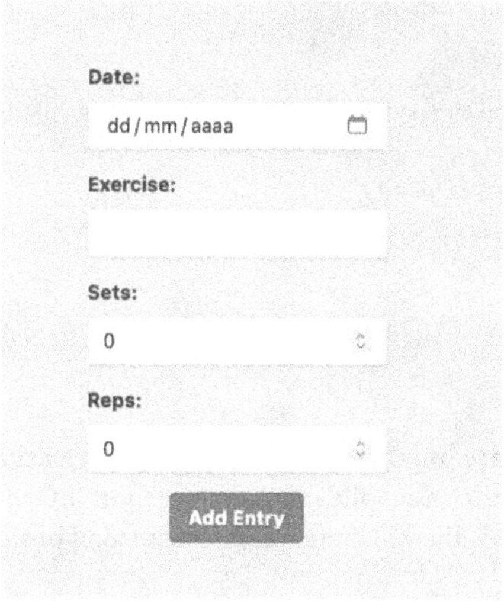

Figure 6.2 – Gym Diary Form UI using a reactive -form

You may be wondering, what is the advantage of using the reactive form and why is it recommended by the Angular community and team? Next, we'll see how to use the form's built-in validations and how to integrate them into our reactive form.

Data validation

A good UX practice is to validate the information that users enter in the form as soon as it leaves the filled field. This minimizes user frustration while improving the information that will be sent to the backend.

Using reactive forms, we can use utility classes created by the Angular team to add validations that are commonly used in forms. Let's improve our project, first in the NewEntryFormReactiveComponent component:

```
. . .
import { FormBuilder, FormGroup, Validators } from '@angular/forms';
. . .
export class NewEntryFormReactiveComponent implements OnInit {
. . .
  ngOnInit() {
    this.entryForm = this.formBuilder.group({
      date: ['', Validators.required],
      exercise: ['', Validators.required],
      sets: ['', [Validators.required, Validators.min(0)]],
      reps: ['', [Validators.required, Validators.min(0)]],
    });
```

```
   }
 newEntry() {
    if (this.entryForm.valid) {
      const newEntry = { ...this.entryForm.value };
      this.exerciseSetsService
        .addNewItem(newEntry)
        .subscribe((entry) => this.router.navigate(['/home']));
    }
  }
}
```

In the preceding example, we are importing the `Validators` package from Angular that will provide the `utility` class for the basic validations of our report. In the `ngOnInit` method where we create the reactive form object, the validations are in the second position of the array that defines the form's fields.

We use the required validation in all fields of the form, and in the `sets` and `reps` fields, we add another validation to guarantee that the number is positive. To add more than one validation, we can add another array with the validations.

Another change we made to our component is that it now checks whether the form is valid before starting the interaction with the backend. We do this by checking the `valid` attribute of the object. Angular automatically updates this field as the user enters data.

In the template file, let's add the error messages for the user:

```
<div
  *ngIf="entryForm.get('date')?.invalid && entryForm.get('date')?.
touched"
  class="mt-1 text-red-500"
>
  Date is required.
</div>
<div
  *ngIf="
    entryForm.get('exercise')?.invalid &&
    entryForm.get('exercise')?.touched
    "
  class="mt-1 text-red-500"
>
  Exercise is required.
</div>
  . . .
```

```
<div
  *ngIf="entryForm.get('sets')?.invalid && entryForm.get('sets')?.
touched"
  class="mt-1 text-red-500"
>
  Sets is required and must be a positive number.
</div>
<div
  *ngIf="entryForm.get('reps')?.invalid && entryForm.get('reps')?.
touched"
  class="mt-1 text-red-500"
>
  Reps is required and must be a positive number.
</div>
<button
  type="submit"
  [disabled]="entryForm.invalid"
  [class.opacity-50]="entryForm.invalid"
>
  Add Entry
</button>
```

To show validation in the template, we use `div` elements with the message we want. To decide whether or not the message will appear, we use the `ngIf` directive, checking the status of the field.

For this, we first get the field using the `GET` method and check the following two properties:

- The `invalid` property checks whether the field is invalid according to what was configured in the component.

- The `touched` property checks whether the user has accessed the field. It is recommended not to show all the validations when the interface is loaded.

In addition to the validations in each field, to improve usability, we changed the **Submission** button by disabling it while the form was invalid and applying the CSS to make it clear to the user.

Running the project, we can see the validations accessing all fields without filling any field.

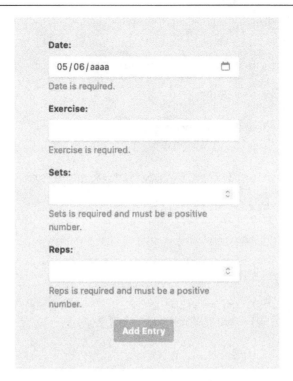

Figure 6.3 – Gym Diary Form UI validations

We've learned how to use Angular's utility classes to perform validation, so let's explore how we can create our own custom validations.

Custom validations

We can expand the use of validations and create custom functions that can even receive parameters to maximize reuse in our projects. To illustrate this, let's create a custom validation to evaluate whether the number of repetitions or sets are multiples of two and three, respectively.

Let's create a new file called custom-validation.ts and add the following function:

```
import { AbstractControl, ValidationErrors, ValidatorFn } from '@
angular/forms';

export function multipleValidator(multiple: number): ValidatorFn {
  return (control: AbstractControl): ValidationErrors | null => {
    const isNotMultiple = control.value % multiple !== 0;
    return isNotMultiple ? { isNotMultiple: { value: control.value } }
: null;
```

```
    };
}
```

For Angular to recognize the form validation function, it must return a new function with the signature described in the `ValidatorFn` interface. This signature defines that it will receive `AbstractControl` and must return an object of type `ValidationErrors` that allows the template to interpret the new type of validation.

Here, we get the input value using `control.value`, and if it is not a multiple of three, we will return the `error` object. Otherwise, we will return `null`, which will indicate to Angular that the value is correct.

To use this function, we are going to refactor our form component as follows:

```
. . .
  ngOnInit() {
    this.entryForm = this.formBuilder.group({
      date: ['', Validators.required],
      exercise: ['', Validators.required],
      sets: [
        '',
        [Validators.required, Validators.min(0), multipleValidator(2)],
      ],
      reps: [
        '',
        [Validators.required, Validators.min(0), multipleValidator(3)],
      ],
    });
}
. . .
```

To use our custom function, we import it from the new file we created and use it in the validation array in the construction of the form object in the same way as standard Angular validations.

Finally, let's change the form template to add the error message:

```
. . .
    <div
      *ngIf="
        entryForm.get('sets')?.errors?.['isNotMultiple'] &&
        entryForm.get('sets')?.touched
      "
      class="mt-1 text-red-500"
    >
      sets is required and must be multiple of 2.
```

```
    </div>
 . . .
    <div
      *ngIf="
        entryForm.get('reps')?.errors?.['isNotMultiple'] &&
        entryForm.get('reps')?.touched
      "
      class="mt-1 text-red-500"
    >
      Reps is required and must be multiple of 3.
    </div>
 . . .
```

We include the new div elements, but to specifically validate the error of multiples of the input, we use the error attribute and in it the new isNotMultiple attribute of our custom function.

We are using this parameter in square brackets because it is defined at runtime and Angular will warn at compile time that it does not exist.

Running our project, we can see the new validations:

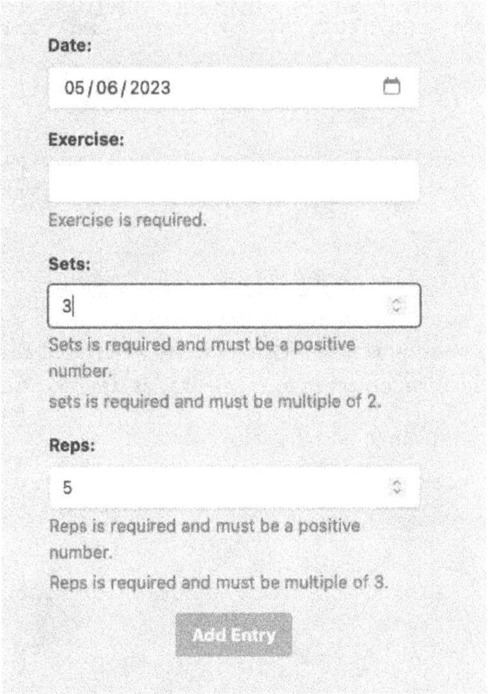

Figure 6.4 – Gym Diary Form UI custom validations

In addition to validations, reactive forms from version 14 of Angular can be better typed to ensure higher productivity and security in the development of your project. We will go over this function in the next section.

Typed reactive forms

In our project, if we look at the types of objects and values, we can see that they are all of the any type. Although functional, it is possible to improve this development experience by better using TypeScript's type checking.

Let's refactor our code in the component as follows:

```
export class NewEntryFormReactiveComponent {
  private formBuilder = inject(FormBuilder);
  private exerciseSetsService = inject(ExerciseSetsService);
  private router = inject(Router);

  public entryForm = this.formBuilder.group({
    date: [new Date(), Validators.required],
    exercise: ['', Validators.required],
    sets: [0, [Validators.required, Validators.min(0),
multipleValidator(2)]],
    reps: [0, [Validators.required, Validators.min(0),
multipleValidator(3)]],
  });

  newEntry() {
    if (this.entryForm.valid) {
      const newEntry = { ...this.entryForm.value };
      this.exerciseSetsService
        .addNewItem(newEntry)
        .subscribe((entry) => this.router.navigate(['/home']));
    }
  }
}
```

We moved the creation of the form object to the construction of the component and set the initialization of the fields with the types that will be accepted by the API. Using Visual Studio Code's IntelliSense, we can see that Angular infers the types and now we have an object very close to the ExerciseSet type.

With this change, however, the addNewItem method threw an error, which is actually a good thing, as it means that we are now using TypeScript's type checking to discover possible bugs that could only appear at runtime. To resolve this issue, we first need to change the service to receive an object that can contain some of the attributes of ExerciseSet.

In the service, change the `addNewItem` method:

```
addNewItem(item: Partial<ExerciseSet>): Observable<ExerciseSet> {
  return this.httpClient.post<ExerciseSet>(this.url, item);
}
```

Here, we use the `Partial` type of TypeScript to inform the function that it can receive an object with part of the interface attributes. Returning to our component, we can see that it still has an error. This happens because it can receive `null` values in the form's attributes.

To resolve this, let's change the `FormBuilder` service to the `NonNullableFormBuilder` type as follows:

```
export class NewEntryFormReactiveComponent {
  . . .
    private formBuilder = inject(NonNullableFormBuilder);
  . . .
}
```

With this change, Angular itself performs this verification. The only requirement is that all the form fields are initialized, which we have already done here.

With that, we have our reactive form working and can now use TypeScript's type-checking more effectively!

Summary

In this chapter, we explored Angular forms and how to use them to improve our user experience and our team's productivity. We learned how to use template forms for simpler requirements and explored how Angular performs the binding between the HTML and the data model using the `ngModel` object.

 We also work with reactive forms, which opens up many possibilities for creating and manipulating forms. Regarding reactive forms, we studied how to apply validations to fields and how to create our own custom validation functions. Finally, we refactored our reactive form to use TypeScript type checking using typed forms.

In the next chapter, we will explore Angular's routing mechanism and the possibilities it can have for our applications.

7

Routes and Routers

A **single-page application (SPA)** is one in which the user originally receives only one index.html page and, from there, all the content of the web application is rendered using JavaScript.

From the user's perspective, however, they are interacting with the application on different interfaces (or pages) such as the login screen, the home page, and the purchase form. Technically, they are all rendered on the index.html page but, for the user, they are different experiences.

The mechanism responsible for this flow of interfaces that the client interacts with in a SPA is the routing engine. The Angular framework has this feature out of the box and, in this chapter, we will explore it in detail.

We will cover the following topics in this chapter:

- Routes and navigation
- Defining an error page and title
- Dynamic routes – wildcards and parameters
- Securing routes – guards
- Optimizing the experience – Resolve

By the end of the chapter, you will be able to use Angular's routing mechanisms to create navigation flows that will improve your users' experience.

Technical requirements

To follow the instructions in this chapter, you'll need the following:

- Visual Studio Code (https://code.visualstudio.com/Download)
- Node.js 18 or higher (https://nodejs.org/en/download/)

The code files for this chapter are available at `https://github.com/PacktPublishing/Angular-Design-Patterns-and-Best-Practices/tree/main/ch7`.

While following this chapter, remember to run the backend of the application found in the `gym-diary-backend` folder with the `npm start` command.

Routes and navigation

Let's improve our project by creating a home page with a simplified menu for our interface, thereby exploring the possibilities we can have with Angular routes. In the command line, we'll use the Angular CLI to create a new module and the component page:

```
ng g m home --routing
```

In the preceding snippet, we first create a new module, and by using the `--routing` parameter, we instruct the Angular CLI to create the module along with the routing file. The following command creates the component we are working on:

```
ng g c home
```

For more details about the Angular CLI and modules, you can refer to *Chapter 2, Organizing Your Application*.

First, let's create the template in the HTML file of the component we just created:

```html
<div class="flex h-screen">
  <aside class="w-1/6 bg-blue-500 text-white">
    <nav class="mt-8">
      <ul class="flex flex-col items-center space-y-4">
        <li>
          <a class="flex items-center space-x-2 text-white">
            <span>Diary</span>
          </a>
        </li>
        <li>
          <a class="flex items-center space-x-2 text-white">
            <span>New Entry</span>
          </a>
        </li>
      </ul>
    </nav>
  </aside>
  <main class="flex-1 bg-gray-200 p-4">
    <router-outlet></router-outlet>
  </main>
</div>
```

In this template example, we are using the `<aside>` and `<main>` HTML elements to create the menu and the area where the selected pages will be projected. For this purpose, we are using the `<router-outlet>` directive to indicate the correct area to Angular.

To make the home page the main page, we need to modify the main routing module of our application in the `app-routing.module.ts` file:

```
. . .
const routes: Routes = [
  { path: '', pathMatch: 'full', redirectTo: 'home' },
  {
    path: 'home',
    loadChildren: () =>
      import('./home/home.module').then((file) => file.HomeModule),
  },
];
. . .
export class AppRoutingModule {}
```

The `routes` array is the main element of the Angular routing mechanism. We define objects in it that correspond to the routes our users will have access to. In this example, we defined that the root route (`"/"`) of our application will redirect the user to the `home` route using the `redirectTo` property.

Here, we should use the `pathMatch` property with the `"full"` value. This is because it determines whether the Angular route engine will match the first route that matches the pattern (the default behavior, which is `"prefix"`), or whether it will match the entire route.

In the second object, we are defining the `home` route and loading the Home module lazily. For more details about lazy loading, you can refer to *Chapter 2, Organizing Your Application.*

When running our application, we have the menu and the area where the pages of our workout diary will be displayed.

To include the workout diary on the home page, we need to modify the `HomeRoutingModule` module:

```
import { NgModule } from '@angular/core';
import { RouterModule, Routes } from '@angular/router';
import { HomeComponent } from './home.component';

const routes: Routes = [
  {
    path: '',
    component: HomeComponent,
    children: [
      {
        path: 'diary',
```

```
        loadChildren: () =>
            import('../diary/diary.module').then((file) => file.
DiaryModule),
      },
      {
        path: '',
        redirectTo: 'diary',
        pathMatch: 'full',
      },
    ],
  },
];


@NgModule({
  imports: [RouterModule.forChild(routes)],
  exports: [RouterModule],
})
export class HomeRoutingModule {}
```

In this routes file, similar to the previous one, we define that the main route will direct to the HomeComponent component. However, here, we want the routes and modules to be rendered in the *router outlet* of the component instead of AppModule.

Here, the children property comes into play in which we will define the nested routes for this module. Since we want to use DiaryComponent, we are performing lazy loading of its module. This follows the Angular best practice of separating functional modules in the application.

Now, when running our application again, we have the diary page back.

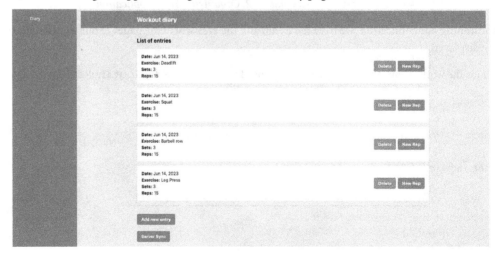

Figure 7.1 – Gym Diary home page with Diary

To conclude this session, let's add the links for the new exercise entry in the Home template. Make the following modification:

```
<li>
  <a routerLink="./diary" class="flex items-center space-x-2 text-
white">
    <span>Diary</span>
  </a>
</li>
<li>
  <a routerLink="./diary/new-reactive" class="flex items-center
space-x-2 text-white">
    <span>New Entry</span>
  </a>
</li>
```

We are using the Angular `routerLink` directive to create the link in the template, specifying the URL it should navigate to.

An important detail to note is that we are using the relative path of the project to create the link using `./`. Since the entry form route is located in the diary module, Angular interprets that the module has already been loaded and allows the link without requiring an additional declaration in the `HomeRoutingModule` component.

In the next section, let's explore how to handle a scenario in which the user enters a date that does not exist.

Defining an error page and title

In our current project, if the user enters a path that does not have a mapped route, they will be faced with a blank screen. This is not a good **user experience** (**UX**) practice; ideally, we need to handle this error by presenting an error page for it to be redirected to the correct page.

First, let's create the component using the Angular CLI:

```
ng generate component ErrorPage
```

Here, we are creating the component directly in `AppModule` because we want to give this treatment to our entire system and not to a specific functional module.

Let's create the template for this component with the error message:

```
<div class="flex h-screen flex-col items-center justify-center">
  <h1 class="mb-4 text-6xl font-bold text-red-500">Oops!</h1>
  <h2 class="mb-2 text-3xl font-bold text-gray-800">Looks like you're
lost!</h2>
```

```
  <p class="mb-6 text-gray-600">
    We couldn't find the page you're looking for.
  </p>
  <p class="text-gray-600">
    But don't worry! Go back to the Gym Diary and continue your
progress!
  </p>
  <a
    routerLink="/home"
    class="mt-4 rounded bg-blue-500 px-4 py-2 font-bold text-white
hover:bg-blue-600"
  >
    Go back to the Gym Diary
  </a>
</div>
```

Note that we have the link to the home page as a call to action for the user to return to the home page.

The next step is to update the `AppRoutingModule` routes file:

```
. . .
import { ErrorPageComponent } from './error-page/error-page.
component';
const routes: Routes = [
  { path: '', pathMatch: 'full', redirectTo: 'home' },
  {
    path: 'home',
    loadChildren: () =>
      import('./home/home.module').then((file) => file.HomeModule),
  },
  { path: 'error', component: ErrorPageComponent },
  { path: '**', redirectTo: '/error' },
];
. . .
```

At this point, Angular will do its job. Just by defining the error page route and then creating another entry in the array, we have defined the `'**'` path and redirected it to the error route.

When we run our project, if the user enters an incorrect page, the following message will be displayed:

Figure 7.2 – Incorrect route error page

Another point that we can improve in our application is the title of the page in the **Browser** tab.

For this, we can once again use Angular's routing mechanisms. In `DiaryRoutingModule`, we need to change the following code snippet:

```
. . .
const routes: Routes = [
  {
    path: '',
    component: DiaryComponent,
    title: 'Diary',
  },
  {
    path: 'new-template',
    component: NewEntryFormTemplateComponent,
  },
  {
    path: 'new-reactive',
    component: NewEntryFormReactiveComponent,
    title: 'Entry Form',
  },
];
. . .
```

To change the title, we just need to inform the `title` property in the route definition. Another approach that is possible (but longer) is to use Angular's `Title` service.

Let's exemplify this in the `NewEntryFormTemplateComponent` component:

```
import { Title } from '@angular/platform-browser';
. . .
export class NewEntryFormTemplateComponent implements OnInit {
. . .
  private titleService = inject(Title);
. . .
  ngOnInit(): void {
    this.titleService.setTitle('Template Form');
  }
. . .
}
```

After injecting the `Title` service, we are using it in the `OnInit` lifecycle hook. Although the route approach is much simpler and more intuitive, the `Title` service can be used if the title can change dynamically.

We will now learn how to pass information from one route to another in the next section.

Dynamic routes – wildcards and parameters

We want to change the function of the **New Rep** button so that instead of adding a rep to the entry, the user can actually edit the entry, opening the form with the data filled in.

First, let's add a new method to the `ExerciseSetsService` service:

```
export class ExerciseSetsService {
  . . .
  updateItem(id: string, item: Partial<ExerciseSet>):
Observable<ExerciseSet> {
    return this.httpClient.put<ExerciseSet>(`${this.url}/${id}`,
item);
  }
  getItem(id: string): Observable<ExerciseSet> {
    return this.httpClient.get<ExerciseSet>(`${this.url}/${id}`);
  }
}
```

In addition to creating the new method by getting a specific item, we also prepared the `update` method to accept `Partial` of the `ExerciseSet` object.

The form for editing the diary entry will be the same as for adding a new entry, with the difference that it will be filled in and will call the `update` method. So, let's reuse the `NewEntryFormReactiveComponent` component for this.

We'll start by editing the `DiaryRoutingModule` routes file:

```
const routes: Routes = [
  . . .
  . . .
  {
    path: 'entry',
    component: NewEntryFormReactiveComponent,
    title: 'Entry Form',
  },
  {
    path: 'entry/:id',
    component: NewEntryFormReactiveComponent,
    title: 'Edit Entry',
  },
];
```

In the `route` array, we change the route of the new form to `entry` and create the `entry/:id` route.

This route is pointing to the same component, but note that `:id` tells Angular that it is a dynamic route – that is, it will receive a variable value that must be directed to the route.

With this change, we need to refactor some parts of our application. In the `HomeComponent` menu, let's adjust the application route:

```
<li>
  <a
    routerLink="./diary/entry"
    class="flex items-center space-x-2 text-white"
  >
    <span>New Entry</span>
  </a>
</li>
```

We also need to adjust the journal and input components to call the new route instead of increasing the number of repetitions. In the `EntryItemComponent` component, we are going to adjust the component's method and `Output` instances:

```
export class EntryItemComponent {
  @Input('exercise-set') exerciseSet!: ExerciseSet;
  @Output() editEvent = new EventEmitter<ExerciseSet>();
  @Output() deleteEvent = new EventEmitter<string>();

  delete() {
    this.deleteEvent.emit(this.exerciseSet.id);
```

```
  }

  editEntry() {
    this.editEvent.emit(this.exerciseSet);
  }
}
```

Here, we remove the treatment and just emit the event. In the template, we will adjust the HTML content:

```
. . .
<button
  class="rounded bg-blue-500 px-4 py-2 font-bold text-white hover:bg-
blue-700"
  (click)="editEntry()"
>
  Edit
</button>
. . .
```

We will also adjust the `ListEntriesComponent` component to properly propagate `editEvent`:

```
export class ListEntriesComponent {
  @Input() exerciseList!: ExerciseSetList;
  @Output() editEvent = new EventEmitter<ExerciseSet>();
  @Output() deleteEvent = new EventEmitter<string>();
. . .
}
<app-entry-item
  [exercise-set]="item"
  (deleteEvent)="deleteEvent.emit($event)"
  (editEvent)="editEvent.emit($event)"
/>
```

We'll make a small change to the diary to reflect the new route. We'll do this in the template first:

```
<app-list-entries
  [exerciseList]="exerciseList"
  (deleteEvent)="deleteItem($event)"
  (editEvent)="editEntry($event)"
/>
```

In the component, we will change the newRep method, which, in addition to the name change, will redirect to the new route:

```
addExercise(newSet: ExerciseSet) {
  this.router.navigate(['/home/diary/entry']);
}
deleteItem(id: string) {
  this.exerciseSetsService.deleteItem(id).subscribe();
}
editEntry(updateSet: ExerciseSet) {
  const id = updateSet.id ?? '';
  this.router.navigate([`/home/diary/entry/${id}`]);
}
```

To redirect to the new route, we are doing string interpolation to include id that was emitted by the output of the list item. Finally, let's focus our attention on the form. In the NewEntryFormReactiveComponent component, let's adjust the button label in the template:

```
<button
  type="submit"
  [disabled]="entryForm.invalid"
  [class.opacity-50]="entryForm.invalid"
  class="rounded bg-blue-500 px-4 py-2 font-bold text-white hover:bg-blue-700"
>
  Add Entry
</button>
```

In the NewEntryFormReactiveComponent component, we will adapt it to now be the form for creating and editing entries in our application:

```
. . .
export class NewEntryFormReactiveComponent implements OnInit {
. . .
  private route = inject(ActivatedRoute);
  private entryId?: string | null;
. . .
  ngOnInit(): void {
    this.entryId = this.route.snapshot.paramMap.get('id');
    if (this.entryId) {
      this.exerciseSetsService
        .getItem(this.entryId)
        .subscribe((entry) => this.updateForm(entry));
    }
  }
```

```
updateForm(entry: ExerciseSet): void {
  let { id: _, ...entryForm } = entry;
  this.entryForm.setValue(entryForm);
}
. . .
}
```

In the example, we use the `OnInit` lifecycle hook to configure the form according to the route it was called. For this, Angular has a service called `ActivatedRoute`.

In the `ngOnInit` method, we capture the parameter of the route that called our application and, if the component receives the ID, it will fetch the entry from the backend and update the form according to the return.

One detail here is that we are using the destructuring assignment to remove the `id` field from the object because it does not exist in the form's data model.

In the same component, we need to change the recording of the diary entry:

```
newEntry() {
  if (this.entryForm.valid) {
    const newEntry = { ...this.entryForm.value };
    if (this.entryId) {
      this.exerciseSetsService
        .updateItem(this.entryId, newEntry)
        .subscribe((entry) => this.router.navigate(['/home']));
    } else {
      this.exerciseSetsService
        .addNewItem(newEntry)
        .subscribe((entry) => this.router.navigate(['/home']));
    }
  }
}
```

In the `newEntry` method, if the component has received the object's `id` via the route, it will behave as an edition and call the corresponding method of the `exerciseSetsService` service.

When we run the project, we now have the input edit form.

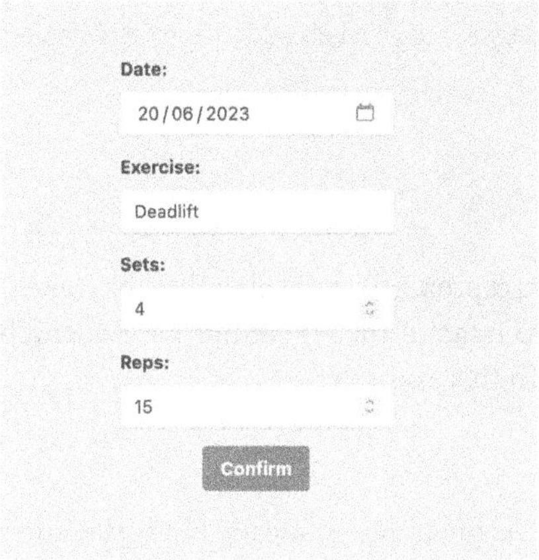

Figure 7.3 – Gym Diary edit entry form

From version 16 of Angular, we have an improvement in the use of route parameters. In addition to the `ActivatedRoute` service, we can map the inputs of page components directly to route variables in our applications.

Let's refactor our example to this; first, change the main routing module, `AppRoutingModule`:

```
. . .
@NgModule({
  imports: [
    RouterModule.forRoot(routes, {
      bindToComponentInputs: true,
    }),
  ],
  exports: [RouterModule],
})
export class AppRoutingModule {}
```

To use this resource, we need to add the `bindToComponentInputs` attribute in the general configuration of the application's route.

In our form page, we will refactor as follows:

```
export class NewEntryFormReactiveComponent implements OnInit {
  @Input('id') entryId?: string;
  . . .
  ngOnInit(): void {
    if (this.entryId) {
```

```
        this.exerciseSetsService
          .getItem(this.entryId)
          .subscribe((entry) => this.updateForm(entry));
    }
  }
  . . .
}
```

We create `Input` for the `entryId` property and define that the route's wildcard variable will be `id`. We did this to prevent needing to refactor the rest of the component, but we could also change the property name to also be `id`, as in this example:

```
@Input() id?: string;
```

The important thing here is that Angular automatically binds the information that comes from the route in the attribute, simplifying even more the passing of parameters via the URL to the component.

In the next section, we will learn how to protect the route from being incorrectly accessed by studying route guards.

Securing routes – guards

So far, we've seen how to take data through the route to determine the behavior of a `page` component. However, the routing created in Angular is versatile and also allows you to shape the customer's journey by conditioning resources based on a business rule.

To illustrate this feature, we are going to create a login screen with a simplified authentication mechanism. To create the components, we are going to use the Angular CLI.

At the command prompt of your operating system, use the following commands:

```
ng g m login --routing
ng g c login
ng g s login/auth
```

The first command creates a `Login` module with the `routes` file. The second creates the `login` page component and, finally, we have the service that will manage the interaction with the authentication of our backend.

In the `Login` module, we will configure the dependencies of the new module:

```
. . .
@NgModule({
  declarations: [
    LoginComponent
  ],
```

```
    imports: [
      CommonModule,
      LoginRoutingModule,
      ReactiveFormsModule
    ]
  })
  export class LoginModule { }
```

Next, let's add the new module to `AppRoutingModule`:

```
const routes: Routes = [
  { path: '', pathMatch: 'full', redirectTo: 'home' },
  {
    path: 'home',
    loadChildren: () =>
      import('./home/home.module').then((file) => file.HomeModule),
  },
  {
    path: 'login',
    loadChildren: () =>
      import('./login/login.module').then((file) => file.LoginModule),
  },
  { path: 'error', component: ErrorPageComponent },
  { path: '**', redirectTo: '/error' },
];
```

In the `LoginRoutingModule` module, we will configure the component we created:

```
const routes: Routes = [
  { path: '', component: LoginComponent },
];

@NgModule({
  imports: [RouterModule.forChild(routes)],
  exports: [RouterModule]
})
export class LoginRoutingModule { }
```

To simplify the handling of the request and response payload of our authentication service, let's create an interface with the new types:

```
export interface LoginForm {
  username: string;
  password: string;
}
```

```
export interface Token {
  access_token: string;
}
```

The LoginForm interface corresponds to the data that we are going to send and the Token interface is the API return, which is basically the access token that the application will send the client's JWT.

With the interface created, let's create a service that will orchestrate the interaction with the backend:

```
export class AuthService {
  private httpClient = inject(HttpClient);
  private url = 'http://localhost:3000/auth/login';
  private token?: Token;

  login(loginForm: Partial<LoginForm>): Observable<Token> {
    return this.httpClient
      .post<Token>(this.url, loginForm)
      .pipe(tap((token) => (this.token = token)));
  }
  get isLogged() {
    return this.token ? true : false;
  }
  logout() {
    this.token = undefined;
  }
}
```

In this service, we make the request to the backend using the HttpClient service (for more details, read *Chapter 5, Angular Services and the Singleton Pattern*). We are using the RxJS tap operator so that as soon as the request is successful, it saves the token in a service variable.

It is through this variable that we create the isLogged property, which will be important for controlling the route. With the services created, we can develop the Login page template:

```
<div class="flex justify-center items-center h-screen bg-blue-500">
  <div class="bg-blue-200 rounded shadow p-6">
    <h2 class="text-2xl font-bold text-gray-800 mb-6">Login</h2>
    <form class="space-y-4"
    [formGroup]="loginForm"
    (ngSubmit)="login()"
    >
    <div>
      <label for="username" class="text-gray-700">Username</label>
      <input type="text" id="username" class="block w-full rounded
border-gray-300 p-2 focus:border-blue-500 focus:outline-none"
```

```
formControlName="username">
    </div>
    <div>
      <label for="password" class="text-gray-700">Password</label>
      <input type="password" id="password" class="block w-full
rounded border-gray-300 p-2 focus:border-blue-500 focus:outline-none"
formControlName="password">
    </div>
    <div>
      <button
        type="submit"
        class="bg-blue-500 text-white rounded px-4 py-2 w-full"
        [disabled]="loginForm.invalid"
        [class.opacity-50]="loginForm.invalid"
        >Login</button>
    </div>
    </form>
  </div>
</div>
```

When creating Login pages, an important point is to correctly use the HTML input field types for the correct UX treatment and accessibility.

With the template completed, let's develop the component:

```
export class LoginComponent {
  private formBuilder = inject(NonNullableFormBuilder);
  private loginService = inject(AuthService);
  private router = inject(Router);

  public loginForm = this.formBuilder.group({
    username: ['', [Validators.required]],
    password: ['', [Validators.required]],
  });

  login() {
    const loginValue = { ...this.loginForm.value };
    this.loginService.login(loginValue).subscribe({
      next: (_) => {
        this.router.navigate(['/home']);
      },
      error: (e) => alert('User not Found'),
    });
  }
}
```

In this example, we are creating the reactive form, and in the `login` method, we are using the `AuthService` service. Run the project and, in url `/login`, we will have our login screen. To use the screen, we have the username `mario` and password `1234`:

Figure 7.4 – Login page

To create the logout treatment, we will create a link in the `HomeComponent` component menu and create the `logout` method in it, redirecting to the login page:

```
<li>
  <a
    (click)="logout()"
    class="flex items-center space-x-2 text-white"
  >
    <span>Logout</span>
  </a>
</li>
export class HomeComponent {
  private authService = inject(AuthService);
  private router = inject(Router);

  logout() {
    this.authService.logout();
    this.router.navigate(['./login']);
  }
}
```

With the page created, now we need a way to guarantee access to the diary only if the user is logged in. For this type of route checking, we should use Angular's **route guard** feature.

To create it, we can count on the help of the Angular CLI; in the command line, use the following command:

```
ng g guard login/auth
```

A selection list will be presented; choose **CanActivate**. In the new file, let's create the following function:

```
export const authGuard: CanActivateFn = (route, state) => {
  const authService = inject(AuthService);
  const router = inject(Router);

  if (authService.isLogged) {
    return true;
  } else {
    return router.parseUrl('/login');
  }
};
```

Since version 14, the recommended way to create route guards is through functions and not classes.

We are creating the authGuard function that has the CanActivateFn interface, which is a function that expects a Boolean return or an object of the UrlTree class to redirect the user to the indicated route.

In the function, we first inject the AuthService and Router services; notice that the inject function in this context is mandatory because, in a function, we don't have a constructor to inject the services.

With the services configured, we make an if statement evaluating the isLogged service property. We return true if the user is logged in, allowing the route to be navigated. Otherwise, we return an object of the UrlTree class with the login page route.

To use the guard, let's change DiaryRoutingModule:

```
const routes: Routes = [
  {
    path: '',
    component: DiaryComponent,
    title: 'Diary',
    canActivate: [authGuard],
  },
  {
    path: 'new-template',
    component: NewEntryFormTemplateComponent,
  },
  {
    path: 'entry',
```

```
      component: NewEntryFormReactiveComponent,
      title: 'Entry Form',
    },
    {
      path: 'entry/:id',
      component: NewEntryFormReactiveComponent,
      title: 'Edit Entry',
    },
  ];
```

By using the `canActivate` attribute, we can pass one or more route guards.

Running the application, we can see that we are directed to the login page. But if we directly call the `/home/diary/entry` route, we realize that it is not protected. This happens because we set `guard` only on the `/diary` route.

To fix this, we can set the `canActivate` attribute on all routes, but a more effective way would be to change the type of the route to `CanActivateChild`.

Going back to the `route` function, let's change its type:

```
export const authGuard: CanActivateChildFn = (route, state) => {
. . .
};
```

We now need to refactor `DiaryRoutingModule`:

```
const routes: Routes = [
  {
    path: '',
    children: [
      {
        path: '',
        component: DiaryComponent,
        title: 'Diary',
      },
      {
        path: 'new-template',
        component: NewEntryFormTemplateComponent,
      },
      {
        path: 'entry',
        component: NewEntryFormReactiveComponent,
        title: 'Entry Form',
      },
```

```
    {
      path: 'entry/:id',
      component: NewEntryFormReactiveComponent,
      title: 'Edit Entry',
    },
  ],
  canActivateChild: [authGuard],
},
];
```

Here, we are using a component-less route pattern; basically, we create a route without a component and put all the routes as children of it.

Then, we use the `canActivateChild` attribute to call the route's guard, so we don't need to repeat all the routes in this module.

The route guard feature can do more for your application than flow control; we can improve its perceived performance, as we'll see in the next section.

Optimizing the experience – Resolve

Performance is one of the biggest variables that impact the experience and satisfaction of our users; therefore, optimal performance should be a constant goal for the web developer.

Perceived perception is the game we want to win, and we have plenty of options in the Angular ecosystem. We can load the information that our page will require before it renders and, for that, we will use the Resolveroute saver resource.

Unlike the guard we studied earlier, its purpose is to return information needed by the page being directed by the route.

We will create this guard using the Angular CLI. In your command prompt, use the following command:

```
ng g resolver diary/diary
```

In the new file created, let's change the function that the Angular CLI generated:

```
export const diaryResolver: ResolveFn<ExerciseSetListAPI> = (route,
state) => {
  const exerciseSetsService = inject(ExerciseSetsService);
  return exerciseSetsService.getInitialList();
};
```

The function injects the `ExerciseSetsService` service and returns the observable returned by the `getInitialList` method.

We will configure `DiaryRoutingModule` with this new resolver:

```
{
  path: '',
  component: DiaryComponent,
  title: 'Diary',
  resolve: { diaryApi: diaryResolver },
},
```

We are using the `resolve` property, much like configuring a route guide, with the difference that we associate an object with the function, which will be important for the component to consume the data generated by it.

In the `DiaryComponent` component, we will refactor the component to consume data from the resolver instead of fetching the information from the service directly:

```
. . .
private route = inject(ActivatedRoute);
. . .
  ngOnInit(): void {
    this.route.data.subscribe(({ diaryApi }) => {
      this.exerciseList = diaryApi.items;
    });
  }
. . .
```

The component is now consuming the `data` attribute of the route. It returns an observable that has an object with the `diaryApi` attribute – the same one we configured in the `routes` module.

When we run our project again, we see that the behavior of the screen does not change externally; however, internally, we are fetching information from the gym diary before the component is loaded. This change in our example may have been imperceptible, but in a larger and more complex application, it could be the difference that you and your team are looking for.

It is important to bear in mind that this will not speed up the request to the backend. It will take the same time as before, but the performance perception that your user will have may be impacted.

We will do this same treatment to load the diary entry edit page; in the same `resolve` file, we will create a new function:

```
export const entryResolver: ResolveFn<ExerciseSet> = (route, state) =>
{
  const entryId = route.paramMap.get('id')!;
  const exerciseSetsService = inject(ExerciseSetsService);
  return exerciseSetsService.getItem(entryId);
};
```

The function injects the service but, this time, we are using the `route` parameter to extract the `id` of the entry to load it. This parameter is offered by Angular so that you can extract any attribute from the route in which you will configure the resolver.

In the `route` module, we will add the `resolve` function to the edit route:

```
{
  path: 'entry/:id',
  component: NewEntryFormReactiveComponent,
  title: 'Edit Entry',
  resolve: { entry: entryResolver },
},
```

Now, we need to refactor the component to use the route guard information:

```
private route = inject(ActivatedRoute);
. . .
ngOnInit(): void {
  if (this.entryId) {
    this.route.data.subscribe((({ entry }) => {
      this.updateForm(entry);
    });
  }
}
```

In the same way as we did with the diary page, here, we are replacing the consumption of the service with the consumption of the route.

Summary

In this chapter, we worked with routes and their resources to guide and organize user flows in our application. We learned about the router concept in the Angular framework and created an error page in case a user uses a route that does not exist. We created our edit diary entry page by reusing a form and, with the dynamic route feature, we learned how to capture route data for page setup.

Finally, we learned about the route guards feature, created our simplified login flow, and saw how to optimize the user experience by loading the backend information before the page loads using the guard resolve feature.

In the next chapter, we will learn how to use a resource to streamline our requests to the backend using the interceptor design pattern.

8

Improving Backend Integrations: the Interceptor Pattern

In a **single-page application** (**SPA**), communication with the backend is one of the most common tasks. In *Chapter 5, Angular Services and the Singleton Pattern*, we learned that the Angular component that makes this communication is called `Service`. However, many side tasks are common to all communications with the backend, such as header processing, authentication, and loading.

We could do this sides task on a service-by-service basis, but in addition to being an unproductive activity, the team might not be able to implement some control on the request due to the carelessness or ignorance of a new member of the team.

In order to simplify the development of side tasks for communicating with the backend, the Angular framework implements the interceptor design pattern, which we will explore in this chapter. Here, we will cover the following topics:

- Attaching the token to the request with an interceptor
- Changing the request route
- Creating a loader
- Notifying success
- Measuring the performance of a request

By the end of this chapter, you will be able to create interceptors capable of implicitly performing tasks necessary for your backend communication.

Technical requirements

To follow the instructions in this chapter, you'll need the following:

- Visual Studio Code (https://code.visualstudio.com/Download)
- Node.js 18 or higher (https://nodejs.org/en/download/)

The code files for this chapter are available at https://github.com/PacktPublishing/Angular-Design-Patterns-and-Best-Practices/tree/main/ch8.

While following this chapter, remember to run the backend of the application found in the gym-diary-backend folder with the npm start command.

Attaching the token to the request with an interceptor

So far, our backend doesn't have any kind of authentication control, which doesn't happen (or at least it shouldn't happen) in the real world. The backend was modified to perform authentication, but this was reflected in the frontend because, if we tried to log in, the following error would occur:

```
ERROR Error: Uncaught (in promise): HttpErrorResponse:
{"headers":{"normalizedNames":{},"lazyUpdate":null},"status":401,"sta-
tusText":"Unauthorized","url":"http://localhost:3000/diary","ok":-
false,"name":"HttpErrorResponse","message":"Http failure response
for http://localhost:3000/diary: 401 Unauthorized","error":{"mes-
sage":"Unauthorized","statusCode":401}}
```

This error means that our request was rejected by the server because it was not authorized. That's because our server implements a very common form of security that consists of asking for an authorization token in every request.

This token is created when the user logs in to the application and it must be passed in the header of the HTTP request.

We'll fix this problem first by making a change to the AuthService service:

```
export class AuthService {
  private httpClient = inject(HttpClient);
  private url = 'http://localhost:3000/auth/login';
  #token?: Token;

  login(loginForm: Partial<LoginForm>): Observable<Token> {
    return this.httpClient
      .post<Token>(this.url, loginForm)
      .pipe(tap((token) => (this.#token = token)));
  }
  get isLogged() {
```

```
    return this.#token ? true : false;
  }
  logout() {
    this.#token = undefined;
  }

  get token() {
    return this.#token?.access_token;
  }
}
```

First, we change the access mode of the `token` attribute. We are using the # symbol, which is the way to declare a `private` attribute in standard JavaScript. We want the token to be read by the other `component` but never overwritten, and using the token ensures that this happens even if the consumer class forces manipulation.

We change the class to the new attribute name and, at the end, we create the `token()` accessor method to return the token stored by the service.

We'll refactor the `ExerciseSetsService` service to send the token in the request that returns the diary items:

```
. . .
private authService = inject(AuthService);
private url = 'http://localhost:3000/diary';
getInitialList(): Observable<ExerciseSetListAPI> {
  const headers = new HttpHeaders({
    Authorization: `Bearer ${this.authService.token}`,
  });
  return this.httpClient.get<ExerciseSetListAPI>(this.url, { headers
});
}
. . .
```

Here, we create a header using the accessory class of Angular, `HttpHeaders`, passing the token in the `Authorization` attribute. Then, we pass this header in the `get` method of Angular's `HttpClient` service.

When we run our application again, it works again (**Username** is `mario`, and **Password** is `1234`):

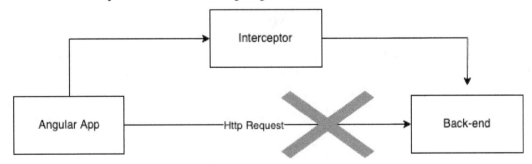

Figure 8.1 – Gym diary home page

This approach has a problem, as we would need to replicate this operation for all of the service's methods, and as our application grows, we would need to remember to do this token handling.

A good software architecture should think about new team members with different backgrounds and even the creation of new teams as the project grows. Therefore, this type of transversal requirement of our system must be treated in a more intelligent way.

Enter **Angular Interceptor**, which is a service of a specific type to handle the HTTP request flow. This component is based on the design pattern of the same name, which aims to change a processing cycle.

Let's illustrate this pattern with the following diagram:

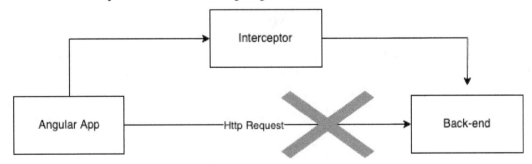

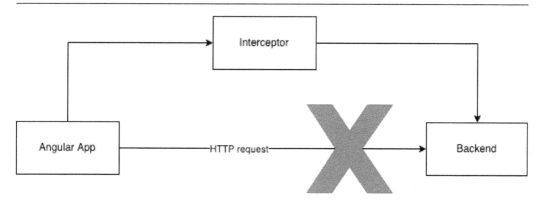

Figure 8.2 – Interceptor design pattern

In this diagram, we have the Angular application that makes an HTTP request to the backend; in the interceptor pattern, we have an Angular service in the middle of the request that can change both the request and the return from the backend.

We will refactor our previous solution to see this pattern in practice. We'll clean up the ExerciseSetsService service by removing the handling from the Authorization header:

```
export class ExerciseSetsService {
  private httpClient = inject(HttpClient);
  private url = 'http://localhost:3000/diary';

  getInitialList(): Observable<ExerciseSetListAPI> {
    return this.httpClient.get<ExerciseSetListAPI>(this.url);
  }
  . . .
}
```

To create the interceptor, we are going to use the Angular CLI for Angular to create the entire boilerplate of the service:

```
ng g interceptor login/auth
```

With the AuthInterceptor service created, let's create our logic to attach the Authorization header:

```
@Injectable()
export class AuthInterceptor implements HttpInterceptor {
  private authService = inject(AuthService);

  intercept(
    request: HttpRequest<unknown>,
    next: HttpHandler
```

```
    ): Observable<HttpEvent<unknown>> {
    const token = this.authService.token;
    if (request.url.includes('auth')) {
      return next.handle(request);
    }
    if (token) {
      const reqAuth = request.clone({
         headers: request.headers.set(`Authorization`, `Bearer
${token}`),
      });
      return next.handle(reqAuth);
    }
    return next.handle(request);
  }
}
```

The first thing we can notice is that the interceptor is a common Angular service, so it has the @Injectable notation; for more details about Angular services, see *Chapter 5, Angular Services and the Singleton Pattern*.

This service implements the HttpInterceptor interface, which requires the class to have the inject method. This method receives the request we want to handle and expects an observable as a return. This signature indicates the characteristic of the interceptor because this class is always in the middle of a flow between the component making the request and the backend.

Therefore, the service receives information from the flow and must return the flow represented by the observable. In our case, we use the AuthService service to get the token. The service cannot attach the token to the login endpoint because that is where we will get the token, so we make an if statement by analyzing which URL the request is using.

If we have a token, we clone the request, but this time, we inform the header with the token. The reason we need to use the clone method to get a new object is that the request object is immutable – that is, it is not possible to change it; we need to create a new one, identical to the old one, but this time, we put the header.

Finally, the flow is returned but, this time, with the new request object. To configure the interceptor, we need to change the AppModule module:

```
@NgModule({
  declarations: [AppComponent, ErrorPageComponent],
  imports: [BrowserModule, AppRoutingModule, HttpClientModule],
  providers: [
    { provide: HTTP_INTERCEPTORS, useClass: AuthInterceptor, multi:
true },
  ],
```

```
  bootstrap: [AppComponent],
})
export class AppModule {}
```

We're including the `AuthInterceptor` service in the `HTTP_INTERCEPTORS` token. This tells the framework to call the service whenever a component uses Angular's `HttpClient` service. The `multi` attribute informs the framework that we can have more than one interceptor because, by default, Angular adds only one.

Running the application again, we can see that it is working now with the addition that all the resources are attaching the header, but implicitly, without the need to change each `HttpClient` call.

Let's explore this feature further with a very common task in our project, which is URL routing in the API call.

Changing the request route

In our project so far, we have two services that make requests to the backend. If we analyze them, we see that they both point directly to the backend URL. This is not a good practice since, as the project scales and grows in complexity, errors can occur by pointing to the wrong URL. In addition to the need to change the host, we will need to change numerous files.

There are a few ways to handle this problem, but a very useful tool for this is the Angular interceptor. Let's see it in practice starting with the Angular CLI, where we are going to create the new interceptor:

```
ng g interceptor shared/host
```

With the generated file, let's create the `intercept` function:

```
@Injectable()
export class HostInterceptor implements HttpInterceptor {
  intercept(
    request: HttpRequest<unknown>,
    next: HttpHandler
  ): Observable<HttpEvent<unknown>> {
    const url = 'http://localhost:3000';
    const resource = request.url;
    if (request.url.includes('http')) {
      return next.handle(request);
    }
    const urlsReq = request.clone({
      url: `${url}/${resource}`,
    });
    return next.handle(urlsReq);
  }
}
```

In this function, we have the URL of the backend and, in the `resource` variable, we receive the original URL of the request that we want to intercept and modify. We use an `if` statement next because we want to avoid errors in case some service needs to call another API directly.

Finally, we create a new request object (this time, with the URL changed) and we pass this new object to the request flow. For this interceptor to be triggered by Angular, we need to add it to the `providers` array of the `AppModule` module:

```
@NgModule({
    declarations: [AppComponent, ErrorPageComponent],
    imports: [BrowserModule, AppRoutingModule, HttpClientModule],
    providers: [
        { provide: HTTP_INTERCEPTORS, useClass: AuthInterceptor, multi:
true },
        { provide: HTTP_INTERCEPTORS, useClass: HostInterceptor, multi:
true },
    ],
    bootstrap: [AppComponent],
})
export class AppModule {}
```

We will refactor our service to only care about the features they need, starting with the `ExerciseSetsService` service:

```
export class ExerciseSetsService {
    private httpClient = inject(HttpClient);
    private url = 'diary';
    . . .
}
```

We follow this with the `Authentication` service:

```
export class AuthService {
    private httpClient = inject(HttpClient);
    private url = 'auth/login';
    . . .
}
```

We can see that if we needed new services or changed the URL, the HTTP requests would not need to be refactored, as we created an interceptor to work on that.

Next, we'll learn how to give our users a better experience if a request takes too long.

Creating a loader

In a frontend project, performance is not only about having faster requests but also improving the user's perception of the application. A blank screen without any feedback signals to the user that the page did not load, that their internet is having a problem, or any other type of negative perception.

That's why we always need to signal that the action the user expects is being performed. One way to show this is a loading indicator, and that's what we're going to do in this session. In the command line of our operating system, we will use the Angular CLI:

```
ng generate component loading-overlay
ng generate service loading-overlay/load
ng generate interceptor loading-overlay/load
```

With that, we created the `overlay` component, the service that will control the loading state, and the interceptor that will control the beginning and end of the loading based on HTTP requests.

Let's create the loading overlay screen in the HTML template of the `LoadingOverlayComponent` component:

```
<div class="fixed inset-0 flex items-center justify-center bg-gray-800
bg-opacity-75 z-50">
  <div class="text-white text-xl">
    Loading...
  </div>
</div>
```

We will implement the `LoadService` service, which will maintain and control the loading state:

```
@Injectable({
  providedIn: 'root',
})
export class LoadService {
  #showLoader = false;

  showLoader() {
    this.#showLoader = true;
  }

  hideLoader() {
    this.#showLoader = false;
  }

  get isLoading() {
    return this.#showLoader;
  }
}
```

We create two methods to turn the loading state on and off and a property to expose this state.

In the load interceptor, we will implement the following:

```
@Injectable()
export class LoadInterceptor implements HttpInterceptor {
  private loadService = inject(LoadService);
  intercept(
    request: HttpRequest<unknown>,
    next: HttpHandler
  ): Observable<HttpEvent<unknown>> {
    if (request.headers.get('X-LOADING') === 'false') {
      return next.handle(request);
    }
    this.loadService.showLoader();
    return next
      .handle(request)
      .pipe(finalize(() => this.loadService.hideLoader()));
  }
}
```

The `intercept` method starts by turning on the loading state and returning requests without modifying anything in them.

However, in the flow of the request, we placed the `finalize` operator from RxJs, which has the characteristic of executing a function when an observable arrives in the complete state – here, turning off the loading state. For more details about RxJS, read *Chapter 9, Exploring Reactivity with RxJS*.

To activate the interceptor, we will add it to `AppModule`:

```
@NgModule({
  declarations: [AppComponent, ErrorPageComponent,
LoadingOverlayComponent],
  imports: [BrowserModule, AppRoutingModule, HttpClientModule],
  providers: [
    { provide: HTTP_INTERCEPTORS, useClass: AuthInterceptor, multi:
true },
    { provide: HTTP_INTERCEPTORS, useClass: HostInterceptor, multi:
true },
    { provide: HTTP_INTERCEPTORS, useClass: LoadInterceptor, multi:
true },
  ],
  bootstrap: [AppComponent],
})
export class AppModule {}
```

We want the overlay to be executed in the application as a whole, so we will include the `overlay` component in the `AppComponent` component:

```
export class AppComponent {
  loadService = inject(LoadService);
  title = 'gym-diary';
}
```

We just need to inject the `LoadService` service because that's where we'll have the loading state.

Finally, let's place the `overlay` component in the HTML template:

```
<app-loading-overlay *ngIf="loadService.isLoading"></app-loading-
overlay>
<router-outlet></router-outlet>
```

Running our application, as we are running it with a backend on our machine, we may not notice the loading screen. However, for these cases, we can use a Chrome feature that simulates a slow 3G network.

Open **Chrome DevTools** and, in the **Network** tab, use the throttling option, as shown in the following figure:

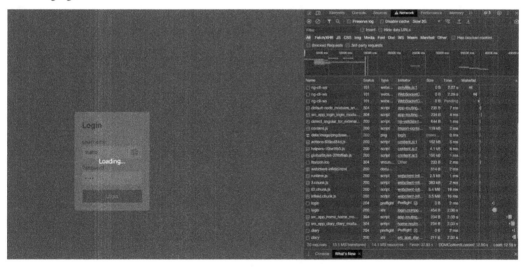

Figure 8.3 – Simulation of a slow 3G network to notice the loading screen

In the next section, we will learn how to notify the success of a backend request to the user.

Notifying success

In addition to the loading screen to inform the user that the system is looking for the information they want, it is important to notify the user after processing an item. We can handle this notification directly from the service or component, but we can also implement it generically and implicitly using interceptors.

We will refactor our application to add this treatment. But first, let's install a library to show the `toaster` component on the screen with an animation. In the command line of our operating system, we will use the following command in the `main` folder of our frontend project:

```
npm install ngx-toastr
```

In order for the package to work, we need to add our CSS to our project by editing the `angular.json` file:

```
. . .
    "build": {
        . . .
        "assets": [
        "src/favicon.ico",
        "src/assets"
        ],
        "styles": ["src/styles.css", "node_modules/ngx-toastr/toastr.
css"],
        . . .
    },
```

For the toaster animations to work, we need to change the `AppModule` module:

```
imports: [
  BrowserAnimationsModule,
  AppRoutingModule,
  HttpClientModule,
  ToastrModule.forRoot(),
],
```

In the `main` module of our application, we are adding the `ToastrModule` module from the library and changing `BrowserModule` to `BrowserAnimationsModule`, which adds Angular animation services used by the library.

With the new package configured, we can proceed with creating the new interceptor using the Angular CLI:

```
ng interceptor notification/notification
```

With the interceptor created, we will change the file with the treatment for the notification:

```
. . .
import { ToastrService } from 'ngx-toastr';

@Injectable()
export class NotificationInterceptor implements HttpInterceptor {
  private toaster = inject(ToastrService);

  intercept(
    request: HttpRequest<unknown>,
    next: HttpHandler
  ): Observable<HttpEvent<unknown>> {
    return next.handle(request).pipe(
      tap((event: HttpEvent<any>) => {
        if (event instanceof HttpResponse && event.status === 201) {
          this.toaster.success('Item Created!');
        }
      })
    );
  }
}
```

As in the *Creating a loader* section, we are using the fact that the request is treated as a flow to use RxJS and its observables to verify the request's characteristics. We are using the `tap` operator, which aims to perform side effects on the request without changing it.

This operator will execute an anonymous function that will check the HTTP event, which brings us to an interesting point. As we are interested in the return of the request, we only select the event of type `HttpResponse` and the event code is `201-Created`.

When we develop an interceptor, we have to remember that it is called in the request and the response, so it is important to use conditionals to execute what we need when we need it.

The last point we need to configure is the main `AppModule` module:

```
providers: [
. . .
  {
    provide: HTTP_INTERCEPTORS,
    useClass: NotificationInterceptor,
    multi: true,
  },
. . .
]
```

Running our project and creating an entry, we notice that the toast appears on the screen with the configured message.

Figure 8.4 – Success notification

Another use for interceptors is to instrument our application to measure performance and stability, which we'll learn about in the next section.

Measuring the performance of a request

As a development team, we must always seek to offer the best experience for our users, and, in addition to developing quality products, we must allow the application to be monitored to maintain quality during production.

There are several tools available on the market, and many of them need some level of instrumentation to accurately measure the user experience. We will develop a simpler telemetry example, but it can be applied to the monitoring tool your team uses.

Using the Angular CLI, we will create a new interceptor:

```
ng g interceptor telemetry/telemetry
```

In the file generated by the Angular CLI, we will develop our interceptor:

```
@Injectable()
export class TelemetryInterceptor implements HttpInterceptor {
  intercept(
    request: HttpRequest<unknown>,
    next: HttpHandler
  ): Observable<HttpEvent<unknown>> {
```

```
    if (request.headers.get('X-TELEMETRY') !== 'true') {
      return next.handle(request);
    }
    const started = Date.now();
    return next.handle(request).pipe(
      finalize(() => {
        const elapsed = Date.now() - started;
        const message = `${request.method} "${request.urlWithParams}"
 in ${elapsed} ms.`;
        console.log(message);
      })
    );
  }
}
```

To illustrate the ability to customize an interceptor, we agree that telemetry will only be used if the request made has a custom header called X-TELEMETRY, and right at the beginning of the function, we do this verification.

As we did in the loader example, we used the finalize operator to measure the performance of the request in a simplified way and presented it in console.log. You could put your telemetry provider call or even your custom backend here.

To exemplify, we use console.log to show the information. As in the other sections, we need to configure the interceptor in the main AppModule module:

```
. . .
providers: [
. . .
  {
    provide: HTTP_INTERCEPTORS,
    useClass: TelemetryInterceptor,
    multi: true,
  },
],
. . .
```

Finally, in the ExerciseSetsService service, we will send the customized header to carry out the telemetry of this request only:

```
. . .
getInitialList(): Observable<ExerciseSetListAPI> {
  const headers = new HttpHeaders().set('X-TELEMETRY', 'true');
  return this.httpClient.get<ExerciseSetListAPI>(this.url, { headers
});
```

```
}
. . .
```

Header passing is a way to configure an interceptor to behave differently depending on the situation.

Running our project, we can see the messages in the browser log:

```
GET "http://localhost:3000/diary" in 5 ms. telemetry.interceptor.
ts:25:16
```

With this development, HTTP requests with the configured header will be logged in `console.log`. You can replace this interceptor with an integration to a telemetry service, improving the monitoring of your application.

Summary

In this chapter, we explored the interceptor feature in Angular and the possibilities that this feature can give our team. We learned how to attach the authentication token to the requests without having to change all the services in our project. We also worked on changing the URL of the request, making our project more flexible to its execution environment.

We also improved our users' experience by creating a loader in case their internet is slow and notifying them on the screen when a new entry is registered in their gym diary. Finally, we created a simple example of telemetry using a custom header to give the team the ability to select which requests are telemetry capable.

In the next chapter, we'll explore RxJS, the most powerful library in the Angular utility belt.

9

Exploring Reactivity with RxJS

In a web application, one of the most challenging tasks is dealing with the asynchronous nature of the web. An application cannot predict when events such as requests to the backend, changing routes, and simple user interactions will happen. Imperative programming in these cases is more complex and susceptible to errors.

The RxJS library that makes up the Angular ecosystem aims to make controlling asynchronous flows simpler using declarative and reactive programming.

In this chapter, we will cover the following topics:

- Observables and operators
- Handling data – transformation operators
- Another way to subscribe – the async pipe
- Connecting information flows – high-order operators
- Optimizing data consumption – filter operators
- How to choose the correct operator

By the end of the chapter, you will be able to create better experiences for your users by integrating their actions with backend requests.

Technical requirements

To follow the instructions in this chapter, you'll need the following:

- Visual Studio Code (https://code.visualstudio.com/Download)
- Node.js 18 or higher (https://nodejs.org/en/download/)

The code files for this chapter are available at https://github.com/PacktPublishing/Angular-Design-Patterns-and-Best-Practices/tree/main/ch9.

During this chapter, remember to run the backend of the application found in the `gym-diary-backend` folder with the `npm start` command.

Observables and operators

Up until this point, we've used observables as a way to capture the data that came from the backend API using the `subscribe` method, but let's take a step back and ask what an observable is and why we don't just use JavaScript promises.

Let's use a table to organize our explanation:

	Single	**Multiple**
Synchronous	Function	Iterator
Asynchronous	Promise	Observable

Table 9.1 – Types of objects by requirement

When we need to perform synchronous processing and expect a return value, we use a function. If we need a collection of synchronous values, we use an object of the `Iterator` type. We use promises when we need the return value of a function, but its processing is asynchronous.

But what can we use for asynchronous processing that does not return a value but a collection of values that can be distributed over time as events? The answer to that need is **an observable**! With this data structure, we can capture a series of events in time and declaratively make our application react to these events.

Regarding the use of promises for HTTP requests, we can use them, but tasks that are verbose and complex to perform when using promises can be done using observables and RxJS instead. We can say that everything a promise can do, an observable is also capable of doing, but vice versa, this becomes complex.

In Angular, most asynchronous events are mapped and controlled by observables. In addition to HTTP requests, user typing, the exchange of routes by the application, and even the life cycle of components are controlled by observables as they are events that occur over time.

We can think of these events as flows of information, and RxJS and the concept of observables can manipulate these flows and make our application react to them. The main resources for manipulating this flow are the RxJS operators, which are functions that receive and return data to this flow.

In the next section, we'll start with the operator that will transform the stream data.

Handling data – transformation operators

In our `DiaryComponent` application component, which renders a list of diary entries, we can notice that our component needs to know the details of the return value taken from the API, in which case the detail is returned in an attribute called `item`.

Let's refactor the service to return just what the component needs already formatted, abstracting the structure of the API.

In the `ExerciseSetsService` service, we will refactor the following methods:

```
import { Observable, map } from 'rxjs';
. . .
export class ExerciseSetsService {
. . .
  getInitialList(): Observable<ExerciseSetList> {
    const headers = new HttpHeaders().set('X-TELEMETRY', 'true');
    return this.httpClient
      .get<ExerciseSetListAPI>(this.url, { headers })
      .pipe(map((api) => api?.items));
  }
  refreshList(): Observable<ExerciseSetList> {
    return this.httpClient
      .get<ExerciseSetListAPI>(this.url)
      .pipe(map((api) => api?.items));
  }
. . .
}
```

In the `getInitialList` and `refreshList` methods of the service, we are calling the `pipe` method of the `Observable` object. This method is fundamental to understanding RxJS since, through it, we can define which operators will act in the flow of information that the observable is enveloping.

The `pipe` method also returns an observable, and when the component calls the `subscribe` method, its result will go through all the operators and deliver the result. For our needs, we are using the `map` operator, which receives the data that the observable is processing and returns the other data that will be used by the `next` operator or, at the end, by the component that made the subscription.

In this case, the operator receives an object of the `ExerciseSetListAPI` type and we will return the item element that is contained in it to the component, which is of the `ExerciseSetList` type. With this change, VS Code, together with Angular's Language Server (for more details on how to configure this, read *Chapter 1, Starting Projects the Right Way*), will point out errors in the `diary.resolver.ts` file. We will correct it as follows:

```
export const diaryResolver: ResolveFn<ExerciseSetList> = (route,
state) => {
```

```
      const exerciseSetsService = inject(ExerciseSetsService);
      return exerciseSetsService.getInitialList();
   };
```

As the service now returns journal entries and no longer the entire structure of the API return, we change the type that the function returns. Note that RxJS uses TypeScript to improve the developer's experience.

In the `DiaryRoutingModule` module, let's refactor the use of the resolver that we fixed:

```
const routes: Routes = [
  {
    path: '',
    children: [
      {
        path: '',
        component: DiaryComponent,
        title: 'Diary',
        resolve: { exerciseList: diaryResolver },
      },
   . . .
  },
];
```

It is important to name your project variables as clearly as possible; in this case, we have changed the `route` attribute to `exerciseList`. What we need to do to finish this task is to refactor the `DiaryComponent` component:

```
export class DiaryComponent implements OnInit {
  . . .
  ngOnInit(): void {
    this.route.data.subscribe(({ exerciseList }) => {
      this.exerciseList = exerciseList;
    });
  }

  newList() {
    this.exerciseSetsService
      .refreshList()
      .subscribe((exerciseList) => (this.exerciseList = exerciseList));
  }
  . . .
}
```

With the use of the `map` operator in the service, now, in the component, we only pass the list of exercises, so the component does not need to know the implementation and the details of the API.

In the next section, we will see another way to subscribe.

Another way to subscribe – the async pipe

To demonstrate the versatility of RxJS in an Angular application, we will perform the task of adding a search for exercises in our backend to the diary entry inclusion form.

Following the good practices of an Angular application, we will create an interface that will represent the exercises. From the command line of the operating system, we will use the Angular CLI:

```
ng g interface diary/interfaces/exercise
```

In the file generated by the Angular CLI, we define the structure of the API return:

```
export interface Exercise {
  id?: string;
  description: string;
}
export type ExerciseList = Array<Exercise>;
export interface ExerciseListAPI {
  hasNext: boolean;
  items: ExerciseList;
}
```

We are using interfaces to define the return of the API and a type to define a list of exercises. The next step is to create the service that will fetch this information, again using the Angular CLI:

```
ng g service diary/services/exercises
```

With the structure of the service created by the Angular CLI, we will complete the logic of the service:

```
export class ExercisesService {
  private httpClient = inject(HttpClient);
  private url = 'exercises';
  getExercises(filter?: string): Observable<ExerciseList> {
    const headers = new HttpHeaders().set('X-LOADING', 'false');
    filter = filter ? `?filter=${filter}` : '';
    return this.httpClient
      .get<ExerciseListAPI>(`${this.url}${filter}`, { headers })
      .pipe(map((api) => api?.items));
  }
}
```

In the service, we are using the `HttpClient` Angular service because we are going to query an API, and we are adding the `X-LOADING` header with `false` to the request because, here, we don't want the loading screen to search for exercises.

If the component passes a filter, we will add the `get` URL. Finally, we are using the `map` operator that we saw in the previous section because we don't want the component to worry about knowing the structure of the API.

With the service created, we can change the `NewEntryFormReactiveComponent` form:

```
export class NewEntryFormReactiveComponent implements OnInit {
. . .
  private exerciseService = inject(ExercisesService);
  public showSuggestions: boolean = false;
  public exercises$ = this.exerciseService.getExercises();
  selectExercise(suggestion: string) {
    this.entryForm.get('exercise')?.setValue(suggestion);
    this.toggleSuggestions(false);
  }
  toggleSuggestions(turnOn: boolean) {
    this.showSuggestions = turnOn;
  }
}
```

Here we are first injecting the service we created and creating an attribute to control when to show the exercises list or not.

The `exercises$` attribute will contain the observable that the service will return. One detail that you may have noticed is the `$` symbol here. Using this postfix for variables and attributes that are observables is a community convention. It is not an obligation, but you will often see this symbol in code bases that use RxJS.

We also created two methods that will be triggered when the user selects an exercise from the list. Let's change the form template:

```
. . .
    <input
      type="text"
      id="exercise"
      name="exercise"
      class="w-full appearance-none rounded border px-3 py-2 leading-
tight text-gray-700 shadow"
      formControlName="exercise"
      (focus)="toggleSuggestions(true)"
    />
    <ul
```

```
        class="absolute z-10 mt-2 w-auto rounded border border-gray-300
    bg-white"
        *ngIf="showSuggestions"
    >
        <li
          *ngFor="let suggestion of exercises$ | async"
          class="cursor-pointer px-3 py-2 hover:bg-blue-500 hover:text-
    white"
          (click)="selectExercise(suggestion.description)"
        >
          {{ suggestion.description }}
        </li>
    </ul>
    . . .
```

In the exercise field, we are adding a list with the ul HTML element, and this list will be presented by the showSuggestions attribute. The focus event of the field will trigger this variable and clicking on the element will call the selectExercise method.

The attention in this code will be on the following directive:

```
*ngFor="let suggestion of exercises$ | async"
```

With the *ngFor directive, we want to iterate over a list, but here, we don't have a list but an observable. How is that possible?

This is the responsibility of the async pipe! What this pipe does in the template is perform a subscription in the observable, take the result of it, which is a list of exercises, and offer the *ngFor directive to the iteration.

Notice that we only got such concise code because, in the service, we are using the map operator to prepare the return of the observable for exactly what the component needs. Another advantage that the async pipe provides is that the framework controls the life cycle of the observable; that is, when the component is destroyed, Angular automatically triggers the unsubscribe method.

We haven't done this treatment so far in the book because the observable generated by an HTTP request is not open after the request is completed, but here we will use observables for other cases that may leave the flow with the observable still open.

It is very important to control the life cycle of the observables that we use; otherwise, we can generate bugs and performance degradation caused by memory leaks. Using the async pipe, this subscription management is done by Angular itself!

In the next section, we will connect different streams using RxJS and the async pipe.

Connecting information flows – high-order operators

As we saw at the beginning of the chapter, there are many uses of observables besides an HTTP request. In our task, we will exemplify this use. In a reactive form, a user typing into a field is treated as an observable.

In our example, let's change the `NewEntryFormReactiveComponent` component:

```
ngOnInit(): void {
  this.entryForm.valueChanges.subscribe((model) => console.
log(model));
  . . .
}
```

Running our application, we can see in the browser's console that typing into any form field triggers an event captured by the `subscribe` method.

Knowing that we can react to user typing events, how do we connect this event to the search for exercise information in the API? We use an operator!

Back in our component, we will refactor the code:

```
public exercises$ = this.entryForm.valueChanges.pipe(
  switchMap((model) => this.exerciseService.getExercises(model?.
exercise))
);
```

We remove the subscription of the `ngOnInit` method from the component and put in the assignment of the `exercises$` observable. However, if we do this, TypeScript and Angular type validation show an error because the template is waiting for a list to perform the iteration.

Enter the `switchMap` operator. We exchange the first flow of events for typing the form with the exercise request flow, passing the `exercise` field of the form model as a filter for the `exerciseService` service.

The result of this is that the `exercises$` observable continues to receive a list of exercises. Executing our project, we notice that we have a list with a typeahead search making the request as we fill in the field, as shown in the following figure.

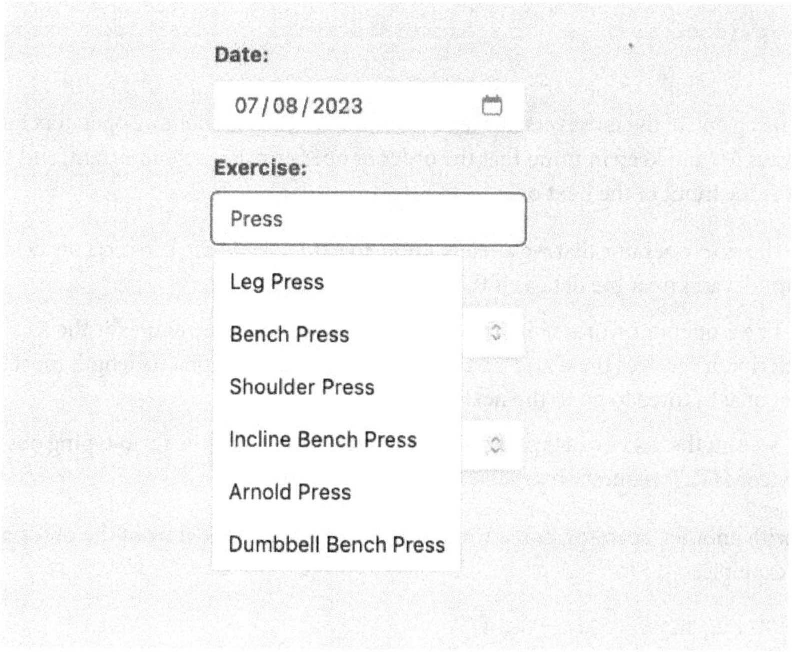

Figure 9.1 – Selection of exercises

The `switchMap` operator is a higher-order observable because it takes an observable as input and returns an observable as output. This is in contrast to the `map` operator, which takes an observable as input and returns a value as output.

With a command, we have our `search` field, but if we look at our browser's **Network** tab, we can see that a request is triggered for every letter we type. We can improve our application's data consumption without harming our user experience, which we will do in the next section.

Optimizing data consumption – filter operators

Our task of creating a typeahead type `search` field is complete, but we can make this functionality more efficient from the point of view of consuming HTTP requests. Here, in our case, if the user types just one letter, we have already started the search for information, but just one letter still results in a very open list.

It would be more interesting for our application to start looking for exercises from the third letter that the user types onward, and we can make the following modification for this behavior:

```
public exercises$ = this.entryForm.valueChanges.pipe(
  map((model) => model?.exercise ?? ''),
  filter((exercise) => exercise.length >= 3),
```

```
    switchMap((exercise) => this.exerciseService.getExercises(exercise))
);
```

Here, we start using one of the most versatile features of RxJS, which is chaining operators for a certain action. We always need to keep in mind that the order of operators is very important, and the output of an operator is the input of the next one:

1.   We use the map operator that we already know to extract only the exercise field from the form model and treat the data as if the field value is undefined.

2.   The filter operator works similarly to the method of the same name for the Array object in JavaScript. It receives the exercise string and we validate that its length must be greater than or equal to three to go to the next operator.

3.   Finally, we run the switchMap high-order operator to switch the form typing observable to the service's HTTP request observable.

We can also, with another operator, add a waiting time for starting the flow of the observable, as in the following example:

```
const DEBOUNCE_TIME = 300;
. . .
public exercises$ = this.entryForm.valueChanges.pipe(
  debounceTime(DEBOUNCE_TIME),
  map((model) => model?.exercise ?? ''),
  filter((exercise) => exercise.length >= 3),
  switchMap((exercise) => this.exerciseService.getExercises(exercise))
);
. . .
```

We added the debounceTime operator to create a delay time for the beginning of the flow, defining the time in milliseconds and with the good practice of using a constant to make the code clearer.

Let's add one last optimization to our code with a new operator:

```
public exercises$ = this.entryForm.valueChanges.pipe(
  debounceTime(DEBOUNCE_TIME),
  map((model) => model?.exercise ?? ''),
  filter((exercise) => exercise.length >= 3),
  distinctUntilChanged(),
  switchMap((exercise) => this.exerciseService.getExercises(exercise))
);
```

The distinctUntilChanged operator checks whether the stream's data, here exercise, has changed from one iteration to another and triggers the next operator only if the value is different, saving even more unnecessary calls to the backend.

We've learned about a few operators, but the library has over 80. In the next section, we'll learn how to navigate the library's documentation.

How to choose the correct operator

The RxJS library has an extensive number of operators that can help simplify your code and handle corner cases of asynchrony and even performance.

You don't need to memorize all the operators and the ones we've seen so far will help you with the most common cases.

The library documentation has a **Decision Tree** page, and we'll learn how to navigate that.

Enter the site (`https://rxjs.dev/operator-decision-tree`) and, here, we will navigate to an operator that we have already studied to exemplify the use of this tool.

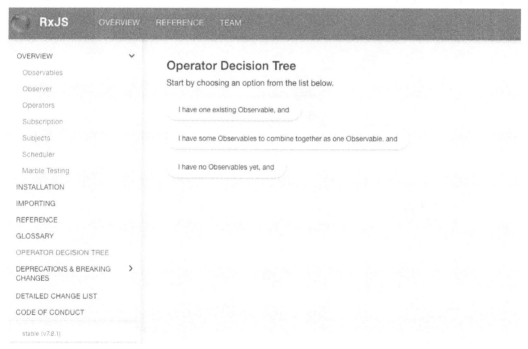

Figure 9.2 – Operator Decision Tree

Let's go back to our form example. We need to fetch the exercise information from what the user's typing – let's assume that we don't know which operator to choose.

We already have an observable, which is the `valueChanges` event in the Angular form, so on the first screen, we will choose the **I have one existing Observable, and** option.

The request to our API is represented by an observable, so on the next screen, we will choose the **I want to start a new Observable for each value** option.

As we want to make a new request for each letter the user types, we want to change one stream for another, so on the next screen, we'll choose **and cancel the previous nested Observable when a new value arrives**.

The exercise search depends on the value that is in the Angular form, so on the final page, we will choose **where the nested Observable is calculated for each value**.

Confirming the selection, the decision tree indicates that the correct operator for this situation is the `switchMap` operator that we are using!

Another thing we need to understand in the RxJS documentation is the marble graph. For this, let's take as an example another operator that we studied in the chapter, the `map` operator here: `https://rxjs.dev/api/index/function/map`.

In addition to the textual explanation, we have the following figure:

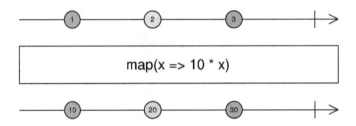

Figure 9.3 – Map operator marble graph (source: https://rxjs.dev/api/index/function/map, MIT license)

As we learned at the beginning of this chapter, RxJS works on information flows, where operators have the function of handling information.

The graph that illustrates this flow uses arrows to represent the passage of time and marbles to represent values.

In the documentation here, then, we see that the `map` operator takes each value emitted and, based on a function, results in a flow with the values transformed by it.

These values are exchanged one by one as soon as they are issued so, in the graph, we can see that the positions of the marbles are same.

This understanding is fundamental to understanding other more complex operators in the library.

Summary

In this chapter, we explored the RxJS library and its basic elements, observables.

We learned what an observable is and how it differs from a promise or a function. With that knowledge, we refactored our project to handle data with the map operator, abstracting the implementation details of the component that will consume the service. We also learned about Angular's async pipe and how it simplifies the management of subscription to an observable, leaving this task to the framework itself to manage.

Finally, we created a typeahead search field using RxJS to search for exercises based on the user's typing event, using operators in order to optimize HTTP calls from our frontend. In the next chapter, we will explore the possibilities of the automated tests that we can do in our Angular application.

Part 3: Architecture and Deployment

In this part, you will learn how to build the architecture of your Angular project to meet the challenges and demands of your users. We will explore the best practices for automated testing using the libraries that the framework uses and we will install Cypress for end-to-end testing. We will understand the micro frontend architecture and how to implement it with Angular. We will use the Azure cloud service to perform the build and deploy our example application and finally understand how to update an Angular application and use features from version 17 onwards such as Angular Signals

This part has the following chapters:

- *Chapter 10, Design for Tests: Best Practices*
- *Chapter 11, Micro Frontend with Angular Elements*
- *Chapter 12, Packaging Everything: Best Practices for Deployment*
- *Chapter 13, The Angular Renaissance*

10
Design for Tests: Best Practices

One of the best practices in a software project, be it a frontend or backend project, is testing. After all, if you and your team don't rigorously test your system, the people who will inevitably test the system and find possible bugs are the users, and we don't want that.

For this reason, it is no wonder that the Angular team has, since the first versions of the framework, been concerned with creating and integrating automated testing tools.

We can notice this with the fact that, by default, the Angular CLI always generates, together with the component, its test files as if saying, "*Hey, buddy, don't forget the unit test!*"

In this chapter, we will explore this topic by covering the following:

- What to test
- Service tests
- Understanding `TestBed`
- Component testing
- E2E tests with Cypress

At the end of the chapter, you will be able to create tests for your components and service, improving the quality of your delivery and your team.

Technical requirements

To follow the instructions in this chapter, you'll need the following:

- Visual Studio Code (`https://code.visualstudio.com/Download`)
- Node.js 18 or higher (`https://nodejs.org/en/download/`)

The code files for this chapter are available at `https://github.com/PacktPublishing/Angular-Design-Patterns-and-Best-Practices/tree/main/ch10`.

During the study of this chapter, remember to run the backend of the application found in the `gym-diary-backend` folder with the `npm start` command.

What to test

Within a software project, we can do several types of tests to ensure the quality of the product. In this discipline, it is very common to categorize tests using a pyramid.

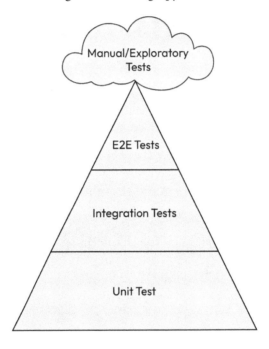

Figure 10.1 – Test pyramid

At the base of the pyramid, we have unit tests, whose objective is to verify the quality of the smallest elements within a software project, such as functions or methods of a class. Due to their narrow scope and atomic nature, they are quickly executed by tools and should ideally make up the majority of an application's tests.

In the middle layer, we have integration tests, which are focused on verifying how the project components interact with each other, being able, for example, to test an API through an HTTP request. Because these tests use more elements and need certain environmental requirements, they are less performant and have a higher execution cost, which is why we see them in smaller quantities compared to unit tests.

At the top of the pyramid, we have **end-to-end tests** (**E2E tests**), which validate the system from the user's point of view, emulating their actions and behaviors. These tests require an almost complete environment, including a database and servers. In addition, they are slower and therefore there are fewer of them compared to the previous ones.

Finally, we have manual and exploratory tests, which are tests performed by quality analysts. Ideally, these tests will serve as a basis for the creation of E2E tests, mainly on new features. As they are run by humans, they are the most expensive, but they are the best for discovering new bugs in new features.

It is important to highlight that no test is better or more important than another. Here, we have the classification by volume of test executions in a period of time. You and your team must identify which tests to prioritize based on the capacity and resources available for your project. These types of tests can be applied to any type of software project, but you must be wondering how we fit this concept into an Angular project.

The concept of manual testing can be applied without tools because what we need is a quality analyst and an application with a complete environment, that is, the backend services responding to our application.

E2E tests are performed by specific tools that simulate user behavior. Up to version 14, Angular already had a built-in tool called **Protractor**, but the Angular team no longer recommends it because there are more modern, faster alternatives. In this chapter, we are going to use **Cypress** for this purpose.

Finally, unit tests are performed on the methods of our services and components, verifying their behavior.

In the Angular toolbox, we have two tools for creating and running these tests: Jasmine and Karma. These tools are installed by default when we start a new project.

Jasmine is a testing framework that has several checking functions, in addition to providing the ability to change the functionality of a method or class at runtime with an element called a **spy**. For the execution of unit tests, the Karma tool is used, which has the characteristic of running tests in a browser, giving the team the ability to analyze the behavior of the application in different types of environments. Although rare nowadays, we may have some bugs depending on the browser it runs on.

To use these two tools, we don't need any configuration of our project; we just need to execute the following command in the command line of our operating system:

```
ng test
```

Once we execute the preceding command, we get a compilation error. This happens because, until then, Angular only compiled the files of our components and ignored the test files because they will not be deployed to users in the final version.

Running the test, we notice that we have an error in the `diary.resolver.spec.ts` test file, so let's make a correction:

```
describe('diaryResolver', () => {
  const executeResolver: ResolveFn<ExerciseSetList> = (...
resolverParameters) =>
      TestBed.runInInjectionContext(() => diaryResolver(...
resolverParameters));
  beforeEach(() => {
    TestBed.configureTestingModule({});
```

```
  });
  it('should be created', () => {
    expect(executeResolver).toBeTruthy();
  });
});
```

The test generated by the Angular CLI contains all of Jasmine's boilerplate. In the `describe` function, we define our test case, which is a test group that we will create.

This function has, in the first parameter, a string that represents the name of the test case and will even identify it in reports.

In the second parameter, we have the function where we will have the preparation and the tests. Here, we made a correction because the resolver we want to test returns an object of type `ExerciseSetList` and not a Boolean as it was before.

On the next line, we have the `TestBed` class, which is the most fundamental element of Angular tests.

This framework class has the function of preparing the Angular execution environment for the tests to run. We will see in the following sections its use in different situations.

The `beforeEach` function has the objective of performing some common action before executing the tests.

Finally, the `it` function is where we will create the tests. Inside a `describe` function, we can have numerous functions of the `it type`.

If we run Karma again, the browser will open, and we can follow the execution of the tests:

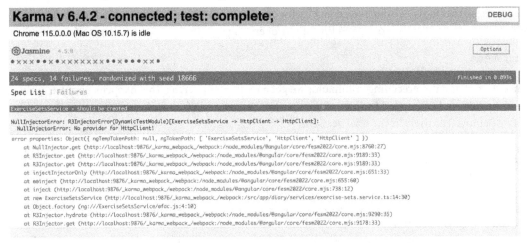

Figure 10.2 – Execution of tests by Karma

As this project already had the tests when we created the elements of our application, we have some broken tests that we will correct in the next sections, but the important thing now is for us to understand how to run the unit tests of our application.

In the next section, we'll learn how to create tests for our project's services.

Service tests

As we studied in detail in *Chapter 5, Angular Services and the Singleton Pattern*, the service that works as a repository of business rules in an Angular application. Consequently, it is crucial for us to develop unit tests for these services. In this section, we will focus on the ExerciseSetsService service to illustrate the Angular unit testing techniques in our project. Let's begin.

In the exercise-sets.service.spec.ts test file, let's start by fixing the tests automatically created by the Angular CLI that are not running correctly:

```
import { TestBed } from '@angular/core/testing';
import { ExerciseSetsService } from './exercise-sets.service';
import { HttpClientTestingModule } from '@angular/common/http/
testing';
  fdescribe('ExerciseSetsService', () => {
    let service: ExerciseSetsService;
    let httpMock: HttpTestingController;

  beforeEach(() => {
    TestBed.configureTestingModule({ imports:
[HttpClientTestingModule] });
    service = TestBed.inject(ExerciseSetsService);
    httpMock = TestBed.inject(HttpTestingController);
  });
  it('should be created', () => {
    expect(service).toBeTruthy();
  });
});
```

As we want to work on service testing, at this time, we replace the describe function with the fdescribe function, so the Karma test runner will only execute this test case. The fdescribe feature is also available for isolating a specific test, in this case replacing the it function with the fit function. To fix the error identified by the Angular compiler, we import the 'HttpClientTestingModule' module in the TestBed component.

We need to understand how Karma, Jasmine, and Angular work together to run tests. Before each test case is defined in it functions, Angular sets up an isolated environment for the tests. This environment has virtually no module configuration at first, as your real application has, and the TestBed component comes into play, where we configure the minimum necessary dependencies for your test to run.

In this service, as it depends on `HttpClient` to perform HTTP requests, we need to import the `HttpClientModule` module to have this dependency. You might be wondering, "But here you are using `HttpClientTestingModule`. Is this correct?" As we will see in the following code, not only will we want to use `HttpClient` but we will also need to simulate HTTP calls, and to make this task easier, the Angular team has prepared a specific module for this type of testing.

With our basic "should be created" test case in place, let's test the methods of the class:

```
it('should use the method getInitialList to return the list of
entries', fakeAsync(() => {
  const fakeBody: ExerciseSetListAPI = {
    hasNext: false,
    items: [
      {
        id: '1',
        date: new Date(),
        exercise: 'Deadlift',
        reps: 15,
        sets: 4,
      },
    ],
  };
  service.getInitialList().subscribe((response) => {
    expect(response).toEqual(fakeBody.items);
  });
  const request = httpMock.expectOne((req) => {
    return req.method === 'GET';
  });
  request.flush(fakeBody);
  tick();
}));
```

As you can see from the preceding code, this service is designed to handle requests related to gym diary entries. In the initial method, `getInitialList`, our objective is to verify whether the service accurately initiates an HTTP request to the backend using the GET method. By creating a new case with the `it` function in the first parameter, we place a description of the test case that will be important for viewing during test execution. The test function, unlike the "should be created" test case, is contained within the `fakeAsync` function created by the Angular team to facilitate the testing of asynchronous methods, such as an HTTP request. Inside the function, we begin to assemble our test. Here, we need to define what the structure of a unit test looks like.

A unit test consists of three parts:

- The test setup, where we prepare all the elements for the tests to take place
- The execution of the method to be executed
- The test assertion, where we compare the execution result with the expected return

In this test case, part of the setup was done in the beforeEach function, but note that, instead, we must put the setup common to all test cases that will be executed to avoid slowdowns in the test cases. In the test in question, we defined a fake return from our server, since the unit tests must be executed independently of the backend service. In the execution phase, we call the service with the getInitialList method.

We call the subscribe method of the observable that the service returns, and inside it, we make the assertion that we expect the return to be equal to the item element of the fakeBody object. Here, the assertion phase can be tricky because, to check the return of this observable, we need to simulate the backend processing of the project.

Enter the Angular HttpTestingController service, with which we can emulate a response from our backend service. Here, we also create an assertion to ensure that our method is calling the API with the GET HTTP verb. In order to simulate the HTTP request , we use the flush method of the service and what we want to send – in this case, the fakebody object. But we need to remember that an HTTP operation is asynchronous so we use the tick function, available within the context of the fakeAsync function, to simulate the time that would pass for an asynchronous execution.

We will create a test for the same service to simulate the creation of a new entry:

```
it('should use the method addNewItem to add a new Entry', fakeAsync(()
=> {
  const fakeBody: ExerciseSet = {
    id: '1',
    date: new Date(),
    exercise: 'Deadlift',
    reps: 15,
    sets: 4,
  };
  service.addNewItem(fakeBody).subscribe((response) => {
    expect(response).toEqual(fakeBody);
  });
  const request = httpMock.expectOne((req) => {
    return req.method === 'POST';
  });
  request.flush(fakeBody);
  tick();
}));
```

We start with the definition of the new test that will appear in Karma and then we create the test function, again within the context of the fakeAsync function.

In the test setup, we define an object called fakeBody with the payload we want to send and make the assertion. In the execution phase of the method we want to test, we call the addNewItem method and place the assertion inside the subscribe function. We perform the assertion of the POST verb, and finally, we simulate the request using the flush and tick functions.

To end this session, let's switch the fdescribe function to the describe function. In the test file of the ExercisesService, AuthInterceptor, and AuthService services, let's make the following change:

```
beforeEach(() => {
  TestBed.configureTestingModule({ imports: [HttpClientTestingModule]
});
  . . .
});
```

As we saw in this section, we need to inform Angular of the test's dependency, that is, declaring HttpClientTestingModule in the configuration of the TestBed component.

We still have to correct the test of the NotificationInterceptor service, which uses an external library as a dependency. We will refactor the notification.interceptor.spec.ts file as follows:

```
describe('NotificationInterceptor', () => {
  beforeEach(() =>
    TestBed.configureTestingModule({
      providers: [
        NotificationInterceptor,
        {
          provide: ToastrService,
          useValue: jasmine.createSpyObj('ToastrService',
['success']),
        },
      ],
    })
  );
  . . .
});
```

In the case of general dependencies that we need to simulate in our tests, we can define the service in the `providers` property in the `TestBed` class definition. But instead of offering the original `ToastrService` class, we declare an object and, using the `useValue` property, it tells Angular which class to provide for the test.

Here, we could create a class that has the same original methods, but better than that, we are using a feature of the Jasmine test framework, which is the spy objects. With them, we can mock entire classes for our tests, thus managing to simulate unit test dependencies.

In the next section, we'll fix all the tests and understand how Angular's `TestBed` component works.

Fixing the tests and understanding TestBed

To better understand the use of `TestBed`, we'll fix the rest of our project's tests by adding dependencies to the test files. We'll start with the `app.component.spec.ts` file and make the fixes as follows:

```
describe('AppComponent', () => {
  beforeEach(async () => {
    await TestBed.configureTestingModule({
    declarations: [AppComponent],
    imports: [RouterTestingModule],
  }).compileComponents();
  });

  it('should create the app', () => {
    const fixture = TestBed.createComponent(AppComponent);
    const app = fixture.componentInstance;
    expect(app).toBeTruthy();
  });
});
```

In this test, we cleaned up the test cases that had already been created by the Angular CLI when we started the project. It has the `router-outlet` component so we need to mock Angular's route services. Like the `HttpClient` service, the Angular team has also prepared a specific module for testing, and so we are importing the `RouterTestingModule` module here.

We'll change the test in the `login.component.spec.ts` file next:

```
beforeEach(() => {
  TestBed.configureTestingModule({
    declarations: [LoginComponent],
    imports: [ReactiveFormsModule],
    providers: [
      AuthService,
      {
```

```
          provide: AuthService,
          useValue: jasmine.createSpyObj('AuthService', ['login']),
        },
      ],
    });
    fixture = TestBed.createComponent(LoginComponent);
    component = fixture.componentInstance;
    fixture.detectChanges();
  });
```

Since the Login component relies on the ReactiveFormsModule module, we also need to import it into our test. Furthermore, the component utilizes the AuthService service, and for our mocking purposes, we employ the useValue property, as demonstrated earlier. In unit testing, it's crucial to concentrate on the component itself, and we achieve this by isolating it through the mocking of its dependencies.

The next test to tune will be for the home.component.spec.ts file:

```
beforeEach(() => {
  TestBed.configureTestingModule({
    declarations: [HomeComponent],
    imports: [RouterTestingModule],
    providers: [
      AuthService,
      {
        provide: AuthService,
        useValue: jasmine.createSpyObj('AuthService', ['logout']),
      },
    ],
  });
  fixture = TestBed.createComponent(HomeComponent);
  component = fixture.componentInstance;
  fixture.detectChanges();
});
```

When testing the Home component, we need to include the 'RouterTestingModule' dependency because we are using route services and we are mocking the 'AuthService' service due to the application's logout action.

Next, let's fix the test for the new-entry-form-template.component.spec.ts file:

```
beforeEach(() => {
  TestBed.configureTestingModule({
    declarations: [NewEntryFormTemplateComponent],
    imports: [FormsModule],
    providers: [
      ExerciseSetsService,
      {
        provide: ExerciseSetsService,
        useValue: jasmine.createSpyObj('ExerciseSetsService',
['addNewItem']),
      },
    ],
  });
  fixture = TestBed.createComponent(NewEntryFormTemplateComponent);
  component = fixture.componentInstance;
  fixture.detectChanges();
});
```

This page employs template-driven form techniques, so for the test run, we include the 'FormsModule' module by importing it. As it only uses the 'ExerciseSetsService' service, we mocked it with the help of the Jasmine framework.

We'll work on testing the new-entry-form-reactive.component.spec page next:

```
beforeEach(() => {
  TestBed.configureTestingModule({
    declarations: [NewEntryFormReactiveComponent],
    imports: [ReactiveFormsModule, RouterTestingModule],
    providers: [
      ExerciseSetsService,
      {
        provide: ExerciseSetsService,
        useValue: jasmine.createSpyObj('ExerciseSetsService', [
          'addNewItem',
          'updateItem',
        ]),
      },
      ExercisesService,
      {
        provide: ExercisesService,
        useValue: jasmine.createSpyObj('ExercisesService',
['getExercises']),
      },
    ],
  });
```

```
    fixture = TestBed.createComponent(NewEntryFormReactiveComponent);
    component = fixture.componentInstance;
    fixture.detectChanges();
  });
```

In *Chapter 9, Exploring Reactivity with RxJS*, we incorporated the search exercise into the form, so in this test case, we need to import the `'ReactiveFormsModule'` and `'RouterTestingModule'` modules. In addition, we need to mock the `'ExerciseSetsService'` and `'ExercisesService'` services.

With this test set, let's go to the last component, `diary.component.spec.ts`:

```
describe('DiaryComponent', () => {
  . . .
  beforeEach(async () => {
    await TestBed.configureTestingModule({
      declarations: [
        DiaryComponent,
        ListEntriesComponent,
        NewItemButtonComponent,
      ],
      imports: [RouterTestingModule],
      providers: [
        ExerciseSetsService,
        {
          provide: ExerciseSetsService,
          useValue: jasmine.createSpyObj('ExerciseSetsService', [
            'deleteItem'
          ]),
        },
      ],
    }).compileComponents();

    fixture = TestBed.createComponent(DiaryComponent);
    component = fixture.componentInstance;
    fixture.detectChanges();
  });
});
```

This component, as it is a smart component in our suggested architecture, needs to declare the components that compose it in your test. Here, they are `DiaryComponent`, `ListEntriesComponent`, and `NewItemButtonComponent`. Finally, we imported the `RouterTestingModule` module into the test setup and mocked up the `ExerciseSetsService` service, thus correcting all the tests in our project.

To understand how `TestBed` works, let's create a test case for our component.

Component testing

Angular component unit tests not only examine logic but also assess the values that will be presented on the screen.

If your application follows the component architecture recommended by the Angular team (more details in *Chapter 4, Components and Pages*), you probably won't have much business logic in your components, delegating it to services.

To exemplify, in this section, we will create tests for some methods of the `DiaryComponent` component.

We will create the test case for the gym diary entry deletion operation and check whether the service's `delete` method is called:

```
describe('DiaryComponent', () => {
    . . .
    let exerciseSetsService: ExerciseSetsService;
    beforeEach(async () => {
    await TestBed.configureTestingModule({
       . . .
    }).compileComponents();
       . . .
      exerciseSetsService = TestBed.inject(ExerciseSetsService);
    });
    it('should call delete method when the button delete is clicked',
fakeAsync(() => {
      exerciseSetsService.deleteItem = jasmine.createSpy().and.
returnValue(of());
      component.deleteItem('1');
      tick();

      expect(exerciseSetsService.deleteItem).
toHaveBeenCalledOnceWith('1');
    }));
});
```

In the preceding code block, we are testing the `DiaryComponent` component, so we mock the service it depends on with `TestBed`. But for this test, we need a reference to this service, and for that, we declare a variable called `exerciseSetsService`. With the `TestBed.inject` method, we assign the value to this variable.

In the test setup, we need to use the `createSpy` function to assign the service's `deleteItem` method because the mock generated by the Jasmine framework does not have the full implementation of the service and therefore does not return the observable that the component is expecting.

In the execution phase, we call the `deleteItem` method of the component.

As this operation is asynchronous, we use the `tick` function to simulate the passage of time.

In the assertion phase, we check that the `exerciseSetsService` service method was called once and with the expected parameter.

Let's test the `editEntry` method next:

```
import { Location } from '@angular/common';
describe('DiaryComponent', () => {
  let location: Location;
  beforeEach(async () => {
    await TestBed.configureTestingModule({
. . .
      imports: [
        RouterTestingModule.withRoutes([
          {
            path: 'home/diary/entry/:id',
            component: NewEntryFormReactiveComponent, },
        ]),
      ]
    }).compileComponents();
    location = TestBed.inject(Location);
  });
  it('should direct to diary entry edit route', fakeAsync(() => {
    const set: ExerciseSet = { date: new Date(), exercise: 'test',
reps: 6, sets: 6, id: '1' };
    component.editEntry(set);
    tick();
    expect(location.path()).toBe('/home/diary/entry/1');
  }));
});
```

To perform the assertion of the route, we are going to use an object of type `Location` – that's why we declare it at the beginning of the test and assign it using the `TestBed` component. Note that we want the `@angular/common` library object and not the browser's default `Location` object. Also, in `TestBed`, we need to declare a route, because as we are in the context of unit testing, Angular does not know the routes available for use.

In the test case, we first create a dummy `ExerciseSet` object and call the `editEntry` method. Again, we use the `tick` function to simulate the passage of time. Finally, in the assertion, we verify that the path is correct. Note that, here, we don't need to create any mock for the router as the `RouterTestingModule` module creates it for us.

In the next section, we will explore E2E testing with the Cypress framework.

E2E tests with Cypress

E2E tests aim to evaluate the system from the user's point of view, simulating operations such as typing in a field, clicking on a button, carrying out the assertion, and evaluating the messages on the screen, just as a user would evaluate whether the action was successful or not.

In the Angular ecosystem, in the past, there was a tool called **Protractor** to help with this type of testing, but it was discontinued by the Angular team in favor of other, more focused open source tools.

Among these new tools, we are going to use one of the most popular ones, called Cypress.

The Cypress framework is a tool that aims to help developers create and run all types of tests in the test pyramid, from unitary to E2E.

Let's see it in action in our project. For that, we need to install and configure it. Follow these steps to install and configure Cypress:

1. We will use the Angular CLI to install and configure Cypress. In the command line of your operating system, run the following command:

   ```
   ng add @cypress/schematic
   ```

2. Following the prompt's instructions, we have created the Cypress files, in addition to adapting `angular.json` with the settings it needs.

3. To run the tool, run the following command at the operating system prompt:

   ```
   ng e2e
   ```

4. The preceding command will run our application as we would with the `ng serve` command and open the tool's interface.

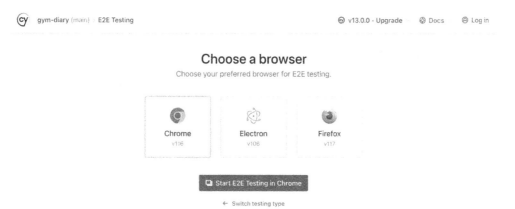

Figure 10.3 – Execution of tests by Cypress

5. Select the desired browser and click on **Start E2E Testing** and we will have the test execution interface.

Notice that we already have a file called `spec.cy.ts`. It was generated by Cypress to exemplify the creation of the test script. Let's go back to Visual Studio Code and check this file:

```
describe('My First Test', () => {
  it('Visits the initial project page', () => {
    cy.visit('/')
    cy.contains('app is running!')
  })
})
```

Unlike Angular, Cypress uses Mocha (`https://mochajs.org/`) as a testing framework. However, in practice, as we can see in the preceding example, it is very similar to the Jasmine framework.

We have the `describe` function to create the test suite and the `it` function to create the test cases. The difference here is the `cy` object, which represents the browser's interface, and with this object, we can perform actions and evaluate the state of the page, from the user's point of view. Here, we use the `visit` method to go to the initial endpoint and we use the `contains` method to evaluate whether the text app is running appears on the page. We are going to delete this file because we are going to create the scripts for our application.

In the same folder as where the previous file was, we will create the `login.cy.ts` file and add the following code:

```
describe('Login Page:', () => {
  it('should login to the diary with the correct credentials.', () =>
{
    cy.visit('/');
    cy.get('#username').type('mario');
    cy.get('#password').type('1234');
    cy.get(':nth-child(3) > .w-full').click();
    cy.contains('Workout diary');
  });
});
```

In this test, we used the `get` method to obtain the page element through CSS queries so that we could act on them. First, we take the `username` and `password` fields and use the `type` method to simulate the user typing in these fields. Then we locate the **Confirm** button and use the `click` method to simulate the mouse click action.

To assert the test, we used the `contains` method to assess whether the diary screen was displayed.

The tricky part of creating this script is the CSS queries needed to get the elements we need. But at this point, Cypress helps us a lot.

By running the test, we can see that there is a target icon at the top of the screen. By clicking on it and selecting the element we want, Cypress will generate the necessary command ready to copy and paste into our script.

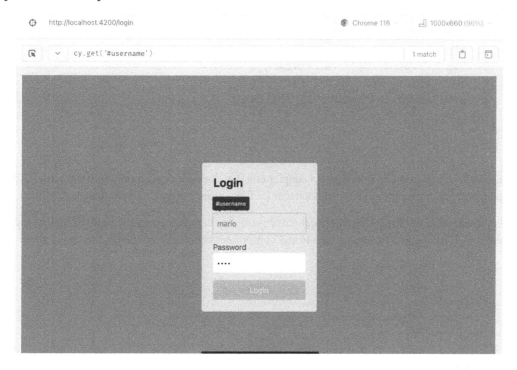

Figure 10.4 – Cypress helping with the CSS query

In this script, however, there is a problem in selecting the button, in addition to the query not being clear to another person reading the test script. If the team needs to change the layout, the test could break unduly.

To avoid this error, let's change the login component template:

```
<button
  type="submit"
  class="w-full rounded bg-blue-500 px-4 py-2 text-white"
  [disabled]="loginForm.invalid"
  [class.opacity-50]="loginForm.invalid"
  data-cy="submit"
>
  Login
</button>
```

With this custom HTML element, we can use the element marked with the `data-cy` attribute for our test:

```
describe('Login Page:', () => {
  it('should login to the diary with the correct credentials.', () =>
{
    cy.visit('/');
    cy.get('#username').type('mario');
    cy.get('#password').type('1234');
    cy.get('[data-cy="submit"]').click();
    cy.contains('Workout diary');
  });
});
```

We replaced the previous CSS query with a simpler one that does not depend on layout elements. Use this good practice in your project templates to facilitate E2E testing and make the test less likely to break.

We'll create an E2E test for the new journal entry form, but first, let's apply the best practice to the templates we'll be using in this test. In the Home component template, we will refactor as follows:

```
<li>
  <a
    routerLink="./diary"
    class="flex items-center space-x-2 text-white"
    data-cy="home-menu"
  >
    <span>Diary</span>
  </a>
</li>
<li>
  <a
    routerLink="./diary/entry"
    class="flex items-center space-x-2 text-white"
    data-cy="new-entry-menu"
  >
    <span>New Entry</span>
  </a>
</li>
<li>
  <a
    (click)="logout()"
    class="flex items-center space-x-2 text-white"
    data-cy="logout-menu"
  >
    <span>Logout</span>
```

```
    </a>
  </li>
```

In the template, we add the `data-cy` HTML element to the items of the menu. Note that as the test is from the user's point of view, we need to simulate how they get to the form.

In the `new-entry-form-reactive.component.html` template, we will change the submit button like so:

```html
<button
  type="submit"
  [disabled]="entryForm.invalid"
  [class.opacity-50]="entryForm.invalid"
  class="rounded bg-blue-500 px-4 py-2 font-bold text-white hover:bg-
blue-700"
  data-cy="submit"
>
  Confirm
</button>
```

As with the login screen, we mark the button with the `data-cy` element to facilitate the development of the E2E test.

With our application better adapted for testing, we will create the `new-entry-form.cy.ts` file in the `cypress/e2e` folder of our workspace and add the following code:

```typescript
describe('New Entry Form:', () => {
  beforeEach(() => {
    cy.visit('/');
    cy.get('#username').type('mario');
    cy.get('#password').type('1234');
    cy.get('[data-cy="submit"]').click();
  });

  it('Should register a new entry in the workout diary', () => {
    cy.get('[data-cy="new-entry-menu"]').click();
    cy.contains('Date');
    cy.get('#date').type('2023-08-08');
    cy.get('#exercise').type('Front Squat');
    cy.get('#sets').type('4');
    cy.get('#reps').type('6');
    cy.get('[data-cy="submit"]').click();
    cy.contains('Item Created!');
  });
});
```

Like Jasmine, the Mocha.js framework also has the `beforeEach` function, but here, instead of setting up the environment with `TestBed`, we use the function to perform the login, since each test where we are simulating the user is necessary for this action.

In the test case of the form, since we are already logged in, we click on the menu of the input form and check whether there is a **Date** label. From then on, we fill in the form fields with data and click on the button. In the assertion phase, we check whether the **Item created** message appears on the screen.

One thing to note is that at no point do we tell the script how long to wait for the backend response, which can vary. This happens because the Cypress framework does this work for us and makes this waiting process transparent to our development.

We will create a test case to evaluate the form validations:

```
it('should validate field information and show the validation
message', () => {
    cy.get('[data-cy="new-entry-menu"]').click();
    cy.contains('Date');
    cy.get('#date').type('2023-08-08');
    cy.get('#exercise').type('Front Squat');
    cy.get('#sets').type('3');
    cy.get('#reps').type('6');
    cy.contains('Sets is required and must be a positive number.');
    cy.contains('sets is required and must be multiple of 2.');
});
```

In this test case, we don't need to worry about the login because the `beforeEach` function performs this function and we work directly on the form. We fill in the fields, but this time, with information that is not valid. In the assertion phase, we check whether the validation messages appear correctly with the `contains` method.

With that, you've learned about Cypress and E2E testing in an Angular application, so let's summarize what we looked at in the chapter.

Summary

In this chapter, we learned how to perform tests in an Angular project. We studied what types of tests there are, their importance, and how to apply them in our daily lives. We worked on our project by first creating tests for the services and looking at how to isolate the dependencies for a unit test. Furthermore, we explored testing HTTP requests using the `HttpClientTestingModule` module. We learned about the `TestBed` component and its important task of setting up the environment for each unit test to run. We also looked at component testing and how to assert components that use routes. Finally, we explored E2E tests with the Cypress tool, which simplifies the creation of scripts that simulate the behavior of our application from the client's point of view.

In the next chapter, we will explore the concept of the micro frontend using the Angular framework.

11

Micro Frontend with Angular Elements

As your application grows and becomes more complex, one team alone is not enough to maintain the growth rate, and new people are needed to handle other parts of the application as they appear. At this point, the architecture of your project needs to evolve, and one possibility is to divide your application into several projects that are integrated as one. This practice was born in the world of backend services and appears in the frontend world under the name of **micro frontends**. In this chapter, we will learn how to apply this principle in an Angular project.

In this chapter, we will cover the following topics:

- Micro frontend – concepts and application
- Slicing your application in the micro frontend
- Creating a micro frontend application with standalone components
- Preparing a page to be loaded by the base application
- Dynamically loading micro frontends

By the end of this chapter, you will be able to assess when it is necessary to use a micro frontend, how to organize your Angular projects, and how to integrate it into a cohesive application.

Technical requirements

To follow the instructions in this chapter, you'll need the following:

- Visual Studio Code (https://code.visualstudio.com/Download)
- Node.js 18 or higher (https://nodejs.org/en/download/)

The code files for this chapter are available at https://github.com/PacktPublishing/Angular-Design-Patterns-and-Best-Practices/tree/main/ch11.

Before you start reading this chapter, remember to run the backend of the application found in the `gym-diary-backend` folder with the `npm start` command.

Micro frontend – concepts and application

In 2014, an article by Martin Fowler and James Lewis (`https://martinfowler.com/articles/microservices.html`) shook the world of development with the formalization of the concept of microservices. Focused on the development of backend services, the idea of dividing a large system (known as a monolith) into small, independent services focused on just one aspect of the business was undoubtedly a milestone for system architecture.

Not long after, this concept was applied to the frontend world, with one of the main articles written by Cam Jackson (`https://martinfowler.com/articles/micro-frontends.html`). The basic idea of the *micro frontend* is the same as its sibling, *microservices*, which consists of dividing a large frontend project (monolith) into small, independent projects focused on one aspect of the business. However, the concerns are different, of course. In microservices, we worry about databases and communication protocols, whereas on the frontend, we need to worry about packet size, accessibility, and user experience.

Let's start by analyzing whether you need to use this type of architecture for your project.

When to use a micro frontend

A big but very true cliché in systems architecture is that there is no silver bullet – that is, there is no one-size-fits-all solution for all problems – and micro frontends cannot escape this cliché. The main advantage of this architecture, before any technical aspect, is its organizational aspect.

When we use the micro frontend, we are separating an independent part focused on one aspect of the business that will be handled by a team specializing in that aspect. With this, your project can scale across different teams dealing with specific subjects that will be integrated into an experience for your user. Each team has autonomy in the delivery cycle of this project, with independence from build, deployment, and testing. Independence can reach a level where teams can work with different versions of Angular and even different frameworks such as React and Vue, although this is not highly recommended, as we will discuss in the next section.

When not to use a micro frontend project

Another software engineering cliché is that there is no free lunch, and choosing to use micro frontends has its costs and challenges.

The first challenge is the performance issue of your frontend. As we saw in *Chapter 1, Starting Projects the Right Way*, in a **single-page application** (**SPA**), the user's browser downloads the application bundle containing the Angular framework code, in addition to the code that your team produced. After this download, the browser interprets the bundle and renders the pages for the user. This entire process must be as quick and efficient as possible because, while it is occurring, the user cannot interact with the screen, causing frustration.

Now imagine this process happening in every part of your system because, to guarantee version and even framework independence, each micro frontend carries its framework engine in the specific version. There are techniques and tools such as webpack's module federation (`https://webpack.js.org/concepts/module-federation/`), but you and your team must evaluate this challenge.

Another care we must take is concerning the user experience and the design of the components on screen because, for them, the components between interfaces must be fundamentally the same to guarantee cohesion in their experience.

This challenge can be overcome by implementing a design system – that is, a single design guide for your company's components, preferably with a library that supports it. An example of a design system is Google's Material Design.

Now that we have a basic understanding of micro frontends, let's move on to the next section, where we will explore how to split our application into micro frontends.

Slicing your application into micro frontends

To maximize gains from the micro frontend architecture and minimize the risks defined in the previous section, we need to create microservices that are as independent as possible and that make sense for your team's organization.

The most common type of project organization is the verticalization of functionalities – that is, for one project you might have an entire user journey, such as a product purchase screen, another project for product registration, and another for the administration module of the application.

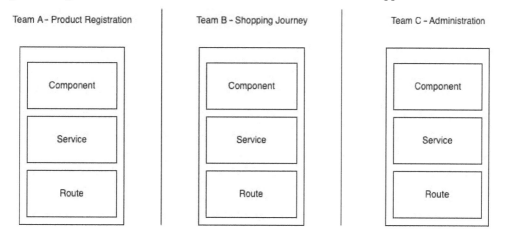

Figure 11.1 – Micro frontend division

This diagram exemplifies the concept of division using an Angular application. In each project, we have all the components for the user experience.

You may be wondering, *"Can I achieve this same separation using Angular modules?"* and the answer is yes, you can. If a team takes care of all the modules for your company's organization or the teams can organize themselves into just one project, you can (and even should) do this.

We need to keep in mind that the reason for dividing your project into micro frontends is to meet an organizational requirement of your project, and teams want to have deployment and development independence.

With the basic concepts in mind, we will exemplify how to implement them in our gym diary project.

Creating a micro frontend application with standalone components

To exemplify the use of the micro frontend architecture in our gym diary, we will create a form to define new exercises for our users. Let's create another Angular project, simulating a new team that will specifically take care of this functionality. In your operating system's command line, use the following command:

```
ng new gym_exercises --skip-git --standalone --routing false --style css
```

We learned about the ng new command in *Chapter 1, Starting Projects the Right Way*, but here we are using some parameters that we haven't seen before. We are using the skip-git parameter because, in this example, we are creating it in the same Git project (which already has the gym-diary and gym-backend projects). The routing parameter is set to false because our project will be loaded in the diary application route, and the style parameter is set to CSS so the Angular CLI does not need to ask what type of styling our project will have.

The biggest difference in this command is standalone, which parameterized our project to create all components as standalone by default. But you might be wondering what a standalone component is. Created from version 15 of Angular, this feature allows you to create a component without using Angular modules (NgModule). Although modules are very important, as we saw in *Chapter 2, Organizing Your Application*, there are cases in which they are not very useful and make the project unnecessarily complicated. A good example of this is in small projects with a limited scope, such as this micro frontend, where we will not have multiple routes or lazy loading.

Before we start creating the exercise form, let's add and configure the Tailwind CSS framework, as we want to have a style compatible with our main application. Inside the created project folder, run the following command from the command line of your operating system:

```
npm install -D tailwindcss postcss autoprefixer
npx tailwindcss init
```

This command will add development dependencies to the project and create configuration files in the Tailwind CSS framework.

In the `tailwind.config.js` file, make the following changes:

```
/** @type {import('tailwindcss').Config} */
module.exports = {
  content: [
    "./src/**/*.{html,ts}",
  ],
  theme: {
    extend: {},
  },
  plugins: [],
}
```

In this file, we are telling Angular that it will apply the Tailwind CSS framework to all HTML files in the `src` folder.

Finally, add the following lines of code to the `app.component.css` file:

```
@tailwind base;
@tailwind components;
@tailwind utilities;
```

With these CSS variables, the component will have access to the `tailwindcss` class.

We will then create a service that will be responsible for interacting with our backend's exercise API. On the command line, we will use the following:

```
ng g service service/Exercises
ng g interface exercise
```

Note a detail of our architecture: we already have a service that queries the exercise API in our main project, but we cannot reuse it here because they are independent projects, and certain code duplication is a cost of this architecture.

Following the best practices, we will create our API as follows:

```
Export interface Exercise {
  id?: string;
  description: string;
}
export type ExerciseList = Array<Exercise>;
export interface ExerciseListAPI {
  hasNext: boolean;
```

```
    items: ExerciseList;
};
```

Here, we are recreating the types that represent the API data. For more details about TypeScript interfaces, you can consult *Chapter 3, TypeScript Patterns for Angular*.

In the created service, we will add interaction with the backend:

```
@Injectable({
  providedIn: 'root',
})
export class ExercisesService {
  private httpClient = inject(HttpClient);

  private url = 'http://localhost:3000/exercises';

  getExercises(): Observable<ExerciseList> {
    return this.httpClient
      .get<ExerciseListAPI>(`${this.url}`)
      .pipe(map((api) => api?.items));
  }

  addExercises(exercises: Partial<Exercise>): Observable<Exercise> {
    return this.httpClient.post<Exercise>(this.url, exercises);
  }
}
```

In the service, we are making HTTP requests to consult exercises and add new ones. For more details about Angular services, you can consult *Chapter 5, Angular Services and the Singleton Pattern*, and *Chapter 9, Exploring Reactivity with RxJS*.

However, we are experiencing an error because we are not importing the HttpClientModule module. But how can we import it if we don't have a module in a standalone component?

In a project without modules, the import happens in the component itself; for services, we have the app.config.ts file, and we will add the import to it:

```
import { ApplicationConfig } from '@angular/core';
import { provideHttpClient } from '@angular/common/http';
export const appConfig: ApplicationConfig = {
  providers: [provideHttpClient()],
};
```

Note that we are importing the `provideHttpClient` provider and not the module. This happens because this provider was created by the Angular team to handle these standalone application cases.

In the main components of the application, we will code its behavior as follows:

```
@Component({
  selector: 'app-root',
  standalone: true,
  imports: [CommonModule, ReactiveFormsModule],
  templateUrl: './app.component.html',
  styleUrls: ['./app.component.css'],
})
export class AppComponent {
  private formBuilder = inject(NonNullableFormBuilder);
  private exerciseService = inject(ExercisesService);

  exerciseList$ = this.exerciseService.getExercises();
  public entryForm = this.formBuilder.group({
    description: ['', Validators.required],
  });

  newExercise() {
    if (this.entryForm.valid) {
      const newExercise = { ...this.entryForm.value };
      this.exerciseService
        .addExercises(newExercise)
        .subscribe(
          (_) => (this.exerciseList$ = this.exerciseService.
  getExercises())
        );
    }
  }
}
```

Let's first highlight the component configuration in the `@Component` decorator metadata. The `standalone` property means that this component can be used directly without being declared in any module. In the `imports` property, we declare its dependencies, which are `CommonModule`, the basis for any Angular component, and `ReactiveFormsModule`, as we will be developing a reactive form (for more details about the form, read *Chapter 6, Handling User Input: Forms*). In the component, we are injecting `NonNullableFormBuilder` and `ExercisesService` and we take the initial list and assign it to the `exerciseList$` attribute. We create the form object with the `formBuilder` service, and finally, we create the `newExercise` method responsible for the **Submit** button.

As we will have the list of exercises in the same form, in the `subscribe` method, we assign the `exerciseList$` attribute again to refresh the list.

To finish the component, let's create its template as follows:

```
<div class="bg-gray-100 flex justify-center items-center min-h-
screen">
  <div class="max-w-md w-full p-6 bg-white rounded-lg shadow-md">
    <h1 class="text-2xl font-bold mb-4">Exercise List</h1>
    <div class="max-h-40 overflow-y-auto mb-4">
      <ul>
        <li class="mb-2" *ngFor="let exercise of exerciseList$ |
async">
          {{ exercise.description }}
        </li>
      </ul>
    </div>
  </div>
</div>
```

In the first part, we have the list of exercises, and here we are using Angular's `async` pipe to subscribe and search the list (for more details, read *Chapter 9, Exploring Reactivity with RxJS*).

In the same template file, we will add the form:

```
<h2 class="text-xl font-semibold mt-6 mb-2">Add Exercise</h2>
  <form [formGroup]="entryForm" (ngSubmit)="newExercise()"
class="space-y-2">
    <div class="mb-4">
      <label for="description" class="mb-2 block font-bold text-gray-
700">Description:</label>
      <input type="text" id="description" name="description" class="w-
full appearance-none rounded border px-3 py-2 leading-tight text-
gray-700 shadow" formControlName="description"/>
      <div *ngIf="entryForm.get('exercise')?.invalid && entryForm.
get('exercise')?.touched" class="mt-1 text-red-500">
        Exercise is required.
      </div>
    </div>
    <div class="flex items-center justify-center">
      <button type="submit" [disabled]="entryForm.invalid" [class.
opacity-50]="entryForm.invalid" class="rounded bg-blue-500 px-4 py-2
font-bold text-white hover:bg-blue-700" >
        Confirm
      </button>
    </div>
  </form>
```

We created a reactive form with just the **Description** field and added simple validation.

By running our application with the ng serve command, we will have the following interface:

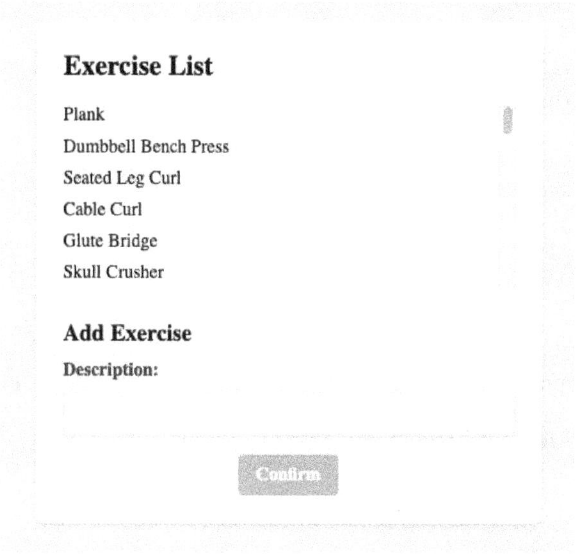

Exercise List

Plank

Dumbbell Bench Press

Seated Leg Curl

Cable Curl

Glute Bridge

Skull Crusher

Add Exercise

Description:

Confirm

Figure 11.2 – Exercise form

With our micro frontend project ready, we can prepare it to be consumed by our main application.

Preparing a page to be loaded by the base application

With our micro frontend project ready, we need to prepare it to be consumed by another application. There are several ways to share micro frontends, from the simplest (and obsolete), with the use of iframes, to more modern, but complex, solutions such as module federation.

In this section, we will use an approach widely used in the market, which is the use of Web Components. Web Components is a specification that aims to standardize components created by different frameworks into a model that can be consumed between them. In other words, by creating an Angular component following this specification, an application created in React or Vue could consume this component. Although Web Components was not created with micro frontend projects in mind, we can see that its definition fits perfectly for what we need.

Like almost everything in the Angular framework, to create this type of component, we don't need to do it manually, as the Angular team created a tool for this: Angular elements. An Angular element component is a common component but *transpiled* to the Web Components standard, packaging not only our code but also the Angular rendering engine, making it framework agnostic.

Let's add it to our `gym_exercises` project on the command line of our operating system with the following command:

```
npm i @angular/elements
```

With the preceding command, we add the `angular/elements` dependency to our project, and to use it, we will make a change to the `angular.json` file:

```json
{
    "type": "anyComponentStyle",
    "maximumWarning": "50kb",
    "maximumError": "50kb"
}
```

The component generated by Angular elements will encapsulate the Tailwind CSS framework, so we need to increase the component size budget a little to avoid errors when building the project.

The next change we must make is to the project's `main.ts` file:

```typescript
import {
  bootstrapApplication,
  createApplication,
} from '@angular/platform-browser';
import { appConfig } from './app/app.config';
import { AppComponent } from './app/app.component';
import { createCustomElement } from '@angular/elements';

(async () => {
  const app = await createApplication(appConfig);

  const element = createCustomElement(AppComponent, {
    injector: app.injector,
  });
  customElements.define('exercise-form', element);
})();
```

This file is responsible for configuring the initialization of an Angular project, and we normally do not change it as we want standard SPA build and execution behavior. However, here, we need to change it to inform Angular that the result of this project will be a web component generated by the Angular elements package. Here, we are configuring the project so that the application will generate a web component whose tag name will be `exercise-form`.

We now need to change the index.html file to understand this new tag so that we can render our micro frontend for testing:

```html
<!DOCTYPE html>
<html lang="en">
  <head>
    <meta charset="utf-8" />
    <title>GymExercises</title>
    <base href="/" />
    <meta name="viewport" content="width=device-width, initial-
scale=1" />
    <link rel="icon" type="image/x-icon" href="favicon.ico" />
  </head>
  <body>
    <exercise-form></exercise-form>
  </body>
</html>
```

Here, we change the default <app-root> Angular component with the Web Components <exercise-form> tag. Our main application will be our micro frontend JavaScript, but the change to index.html will allow you and your team to maintain the micro frontend without needing to load the main project.

We now have a challenge in that, despite creating a web component, the project build is creating it in three files and with hashes, which is correct if our application is not a micro frontend, but in our case, we would like to have all the code in a single file and without the hash. We can do this manually, but the community has a package that automates this treatment: the ngx-build-plus package.

Let's add it to the command line with the help of the Angular CLI:

```
ng add ngx-build-plus
```

To serve this micro frontend, we will use the http-server package, and add it with npm on the command line:

```
npm i http-server
```

Finally, let's create some npm scripts to make running mfe easier. In the package.json file, we will make the following change:

```
"scripts": {
  "ng": "ng",
  "start": "ng serve",
  "build": "ng build --single-bundle  --bundle-styles  --keep-
styles  --output-hashing=none",
```

```
    "serve-mfe": "http-server dist/gym_exercises",
}
```

In the `build` script, we specify our intention to run it, resulting in a single generated file (`--single-bundle`). We also instruct it to retain and encapsulate the CSS (`--bundle-styles --keep-styles`) while ensuring that the generated file's name does not include any type of hash (`--output-hashing=none`).

The `serve-mfe` script uses the `http-server` service to publish the contents of the `dist` folder that will contain the compiled micro frontend.

Let's run our project with the following command and check the micro frontend we created:

```
npm run build
npm run serve-mfe
```

By accessing `http://127.0.0.1:8080`, we can see that our micro frontend application is being generated successfully.

With our micro frontend ready to be consumed, in the next section, we will consume it in the main application.

Dynamically loading micro frontends

Let's prepare our main application gym diary to consume the micro frontend that we prepared previously. To do this, let's start by creating a new module in the application. On the command line, we will use the following Angular CLI commands:

```
ng g m exercise --routing
ng g c exercise/exercise
```

With the preceding commands, we create the module with the generated route file and a component that will be responsible for loading `mfe`.

Let's adjust the `exercise-routing.module.ts` file to target the component:

```
import { NgModule } from '@angular/core';
import { RouterModule, Routes } from '@angular/router';
import { ExerciseComponent } from './exercise/exercise.component';
const routes: Routes = [
  {
    path: '',
    component: ExerciseComponent,
    title: 'Exercise Registry',
  },
];
```

```
@NgModule({
  imports: [RouterModule.forChild(routes)],
  exports: [RouterModule],
})
export class ExerciseRoutingModule {}
```

In the `routes` array, we define a base route for the exercise registration component as it will be loaded via lazy loading.

Next, we will refactor the `home-routing.module.ts` file as follows:

```
. . .
const routes: Routes = [
  {
    path: '',
    component: HomeComponent,
    children: [
      {
        path: 'diary',
        loadChildren: () =>
          import('../diary/diary.module').then((file) => file.
DiaryModule),
      },
      {
        path: 'exercise',
        loadChildren: () =>
          import('../exercise/exercise.module').then(
            (file) => file.ExerciseModule
          ),
      },
      {
        path: '',
        redirectTo: 'diary',
        pathMatch: 'full',
      },
    ],
  },
];
. . .
```

Our `HomePage` module contains the menu, and in this section, we are adding the new module to be loaded in the correct area of the interface.

To finish adding this new module, let's change the `home.component.html` file:

```
. . .
  <li>
    <a
      routerLink="./exercise"
      class="flex items-center space-x-2 text-white"
    >
      <span>Exercise Registry</span>
    </a>
  </li>
. . .
```

With the new menu item added to the home template, we now have the task of including the micro frontend generated in the other project in our interface.

For this, we have a community package called `@angular-extensions` that allows us to load our micro frontend simply using a directive, as we will see later. But first, let's install this dependency in our project using the following command:

`npm i @angular-extensions/elements`

Once installed, we can change the `ExerciseModule` module:

```
import { CUSTOM_ELEMENTS_SCHEMA, NgModule } from '@angular/core';
import { CommonModule } from '@angular/common';

import { ExerciseRoutingModule } from './exercise-routing.module';
import { ExerciseComponent } from './exercise/exercise.component';
import { LazyElementsModule } from '@angular-extensions/elements';

@NgModule({
  declarations: [ExerciseComponent],
  imports: [CommonModule, LazyElementsModule, ExerciseRoutingModule],
  schemas: [CUSTOM_ELEMENTS_SCHEMA],
})
export class ExerciseModule {}
```

In this file, we are first adding the library module called `LazyElementsModule` to have access to the directive that we will use in the component. Furthermore, we have a new property in the metadata called `schemas`. In it, we are informing Angular with the `CUSTOM_ELEMENTS_SCHEMA` token that this module will receive elements from outside the project. By default, Angular checks whether the tag used in the template exists in the project or in the HTML standard, such as the `input` tag.

As we are going to import the `exercise-form` tag defined by our micro frontend here, this attribute will prevent Angular from carrying out this check at the project compile time.

In the `exercise.component.ts` file, we will add a new attribute:

```
import { Component } from '@angular/core';
@Component({
  selector: 'app-exercise',
  templateUrl: './exercise.component.html',
  styleUrls: ['./exercise.component.css'],
})
export class ExerciseComponent {
  elementUrl = 'http://localhost:8080/main.js';
}
```

Here, we are defining the address where the micro frontend's main files will be served.

Finally, let's change the component template:

```
<exercise-form *axLazyElement="elementUrl"> </exercise-form >
```

Here, we are declaring the new `exercise-form` element, and to load it, we use the `axLazyElement` directive assigning the micro frontend address.

To run our project, make sure the micro frontend is being served with the `npm run serve-mfe` command. With everything configured, we can see the result of our work:

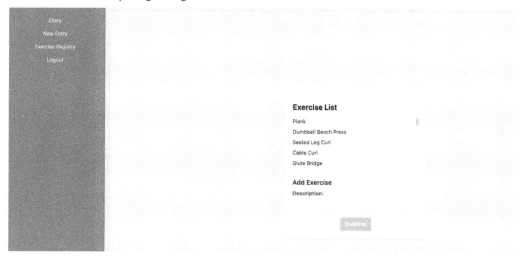

Figure 11.3 – Exercise form dynamically loaded into the main application

Summary

In this chapter, we explored the architecture of micro frontends and how to apply one to an Angular project.

We learned about the concept of the architecture, its advantages, and its trade-offs. We explored how the main reason for opting for this architecture is its flexibility in relation to the organizational structure of each team, as several teams can work on different parts of the frontend project independently.

We also learned how we can ideally divide our application into micro frontends.

With all these concepts, we applied our project by creating a small application using Angular's standalone components feature and preparing it to be loaded by another project using the Angular elements library.

Finally, we performed dynamic loading in our main application with the help of the `@angular-extensions/elements` library.

In the next chapter, we will explore the best practices for deploying an Angular application.

12

Packaging Everything – Best Practices for Deployment

After architecting, developing, and testing your application, it's time to deploy it to your users.

In this chapter, we will learn the best practices for generating production packages and how to use automation tools to maximize the team's productivity and effectiveness at this point in the project.

In this chapter, we will cover the following topics:

- Deploying the backend
- Differentiating environments
- Preparing the production bundle
- Mounting a Docker image with Nginx
- Deploying a page to Azure Static Web Apps

By the end of this chapter, you will be able to use the Angular CLI to generate a package optimized for production and CI/CD tools to automate this process for your team.

Technical requirements

To follow the instructions in this chapter, you'll need the following:

- **Visual Studio Code (VSCode)** (`https://code.visualstudio.com/Download`)
- Node.js 18 or higher (`https://nodejs.org/en/download/`)
- Docker (`https://www.docker.com/`)
- Docker for VSCode (`https://marketplace.visualstudio.com/items?itemName=ms-azuretools.vscode-docker`)

- An Azure account (`https://azure.microsoft.com`)

- The Azure CLI (`https://learn.microsoft.com/en-us/cli/azure/`)

- Azure Functions Core Tools (`https://learn.microsoft.com/en-us/azure/azure-functions/functions-run-local`)

- Azure Tools for VSCode (`https://marketplace.visualstudio.com/items?itemName=ms-vscode.vscode-node-azure-pack`)

- The NestJS CLI (`https://docs.nestjs.com/cli/overview`)

The code files for this chapter are available at `https://github.com/PacktPublishing/Angular-Design-Patterns-and-Best-Practices/tree/main/ch12`.

Deploying the backend

Before preparing our gym diary project for production, let's first upload the backend to a cloud service so that our page has access to the data.

We chose the Azure service for this book, but the concepts in this chapter can also be applied to other cloud services, such as AWS (`https://aws.amazon.com`) and GCP (`https://cloud.google.com`).

The backend of this example does not use a database and was built using the NestJS framework (`https://nestjs.com/`), which actually has an architecture completely inspired by Angular, but for the backend! This framework allows you to add cloud deployment capabilities with Azure. To prepare your backend for deployment, in the command line of your operating system, in the `project` folder (`/gym-diary-backend`), run the following commands:

```
npm install @schematics/angular
nest add @nestjs/azure-func-http
```

The first command installs the Angular Schematic package, which will be used to build the application.

The `nest add` command has the same functionality as Angular's `ng add` command, and here, in addition to installing the dependencies for deployment on Azure, it also configures and creates the necessary files for this task.

With the tools from the *Technical requirements* section installed, we first need to create an Azure Functions project. To do this, let's go to the Azure portal in the **Function App** menu option:

Figure 12.1 – Function App menu option

Azure has several ways to run a backend service, and one of the simplest is through Azure Functions. With it, we can upload our service without needing to configure a server, as the provider will take care of these details.

We then need to perform some basic configurations. To do this, we will click on + **Create**. Once done, we will be presented with the following screen:

Create Function App ···

Create a function app, which lets you group functions as a logical unit for easier management, deployment and sharing of resources. Functions lets you execute your code in a serverless environment without having to first create a VM or publish a web application.

Project Details

Select a subscription to manage deployed resources and costs. Use resource groups like folders to organize and manage all your resources.

Subscription * ⓘ	
Resource Group * ⓘ	(New) Resource group
	Create new

Instance Details

Function App name *	Function App name
	.azurewebsites.net
Do you want to deploy code or container image? *	⦿ Code ◯ Container Image
Runtime stack *	Select a runtime stack
Version *	Select a runtime stack version
Region *	East US

Operating system

The Operating System has been recommended for you based on your selection of runtime stack.

Operating System *	⦿ Linux ◯ Windows

Figure 12.2 – Azure Functions service configuration

In the **Subscription** field, you need to choose your Azure subscription. In the **Resource Group** field, you can select a group that you already have; if you don't have one, you can create a new one and enter its name. The **Function App name** field is important as it will initially be the address of your endpoint. It is possible to buy a specific URL or place this API behind an Azure API gateway (`https://azure.microsoft.com/en-us/products/api-management`), although this is not required for our example. We will deploy directly from the code, so leave **Do you want to deploy code or container image?** as **Code**. The project's runtime stack should be set to **NodeJS**, version **18 LTS**. For the project region, select one close to you, or **East US**, which is the default option. Finally, **Operating System** should be set to **Linux**. The **Hosting options and plans** option should be set to **Consumption (Serverless)** as we do not need any more specific features in this case.

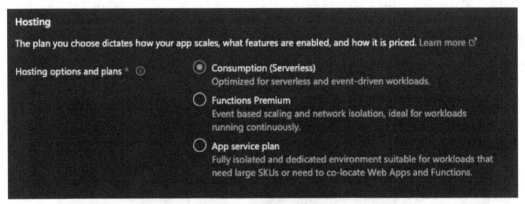

Figure 12.3 – Hosting options and plans

Once we are done filling in all the necessary information, click on **Review + Create**. On the next screen, confirm your information and execute the creation:

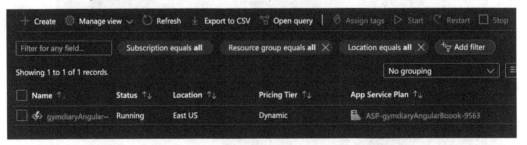

Figure 12.4 – Azure Functions service created

To publish our backend to the created service, we will use the VS plugin. Open the backend project, left-click, and select **Deploy to Function App…**, as shown in the following figure:

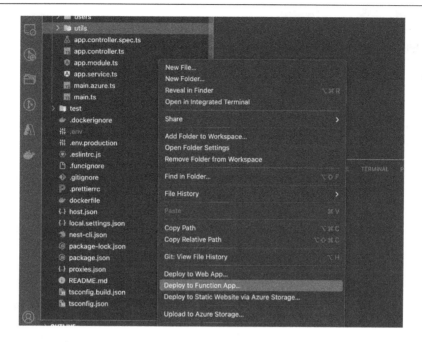

Figure 12.5 – VSCode extension for publishing Azure Functions

The extension will get the list of services created from your account, so select the one we created from the **AZURE** panel.

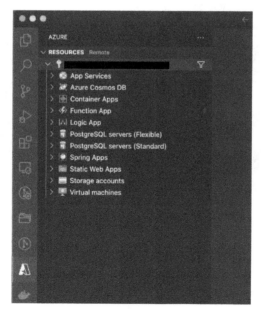

Figure 12.6 – VSCode AZURE panel

After publication, the Azure service will point you to a public URL with your service. Access it in a browser with the `/exercise` endpoint to check whether the service is live.

The return of the published URL should be a list similar to the following:

```
{"items":id":"30","description":"Plank"},{"id":"29","descrip-
tion":"Dumbbell Bench Press"},{"id":"28","description":"Seated
Leg Curl"},{"id":"27","description":"Cable Curl"},{"id":"26","-
description":"Glute Bridge"},{"id":"25","description":"Skull
Crusher"},{"id":"24","description":"Arnold Press"},{"id":"23","-
description":"Inverted Row"},{"id":"22","description":"Chest
Fly"},{"id":"21","description":"Hanging Leg Raise"},{"id":"20","-
description":"Side Lateral Raise"},{"id":"19","description":"-
Front Squat"},{"id":"18","description":"Seated Row"},{"id":"17","-
description":"Romanian Deadlift"},{"id":"16","description":"Bicep
Curl"},{"id":"15","description":"Calf Raise"},{"id":"14","descrip-
tion":"Tricep Dip"},{"id":"13","description":"Push-up"},{"id":"12","-
description":"Leg Curl"},{"id":"11","description":"Incline Bench
Press"},{"id":"10","description":"Hammer Curl"}, {"id":"9","descrip-
tion":"Lunges"},{"id":"8","description":"Dumbbell Curl"},{"id":"7","-
description":"Pull-up"},{"id":"6","description":"Shoulder
Press"},{"id":"5","description":"Bench Press"},{"id":"4","descrip-
tion":"Leg Press"},{"id":"3","description":"Barbell
Row"},{"id":"2","description":"Squat"},{"id":"1","description":"Dead-
lift"}],"hasNext":false}
```

One last configuration we must do is configure the service's CORS to enable our local application to connect to the cloud service. In the Azure console, click on the created service and then on the **CORS** tab and set the **Allowed Origins** field to *****:

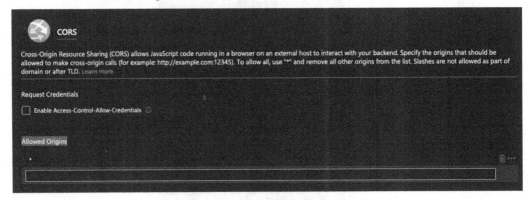

Figure 12.7 – CORS configuration

With our backend service online, we will focus on how to access it from our application in the next section. An important point is to always remember to turn off the service in Azure so as not to incur unnecessary costs when going through this book's examples in your Azure account.

Differentiating environments

After finishing the task of deploying our backend, we need to change our frontend project to make requests to our cloud infrastructure. But here, a problem arises. We want to access our published backend when we are in production, but the team needs to continue accessing the API locally to develop new features in a more practical way. How can we have the best of both worlds?

The answer to this, once again, was thought up by the Angular team and is the creation of configuration files for each development environment.

Until version 14 of Angular, these files were already standard when creating the project (the ng new command). However, to simplify new projects and reduce the learning curve, these files were removed for new projects.

But we shouldn't worry because to add them, we can use the Angular CLI. On the command line, use the following command:

```
ng generate environments
```

After executing the preceding command, the Angular CLI creates the environments folder, and inside it, we have the environment.development.ts and environment.ts files.

These TypeScript files have only one object, and this object is where we will place all the settings that we need to differentiate between production and development environments. We will first change the environment.development.ts file like so:

```
export const environment = {
  production: false,
  apiUrl: 'http://localhost:3000'
};
```

In these objects, we declare a flag to indicate that this is a configuration of the development environment and the URL of our local backend service. We will now change the environment.ts file like so:

```
export const environment = {
  production: true,
  apiUrl: 'https://gymdiaryangularboook.azurewebsites.net/api',
};
```

Here, we are doing the same but indicating the production environment of our application. The backend address will be the one created in the previous section.

To use these files, we must import them and refactor the HostInterceptor service to use it:

```
. . .
import { environment } from 'src/environments/environment';
```

```
@Injectable()
export class HostInterceptor implements HttpInterceptor {
  intercept(
    request: HttpRequest<unknown>,
    next: HttpHandler
  ): Observable<HttpEvent<unknown>> {
    const url = environment.apiUrl;
    . . .
  }
}
```

In our interceptor service, which is responsible for adding the URL to our requests (for more details, see *Chapter 8, Improving Backend Integrations: the Interceptor Pattern*), we use the `environment` object property to determine the URL.

A point of attention here is that we must import the `environment.ts` file for this variable because Angular makes the change when generating the build.

To make it clear which environment we are in, we will change the `AppComponent` component like so:

```
. . .
import { environment } from 'src/environments/environment';
import { ToastrService } from 'ngx-toastr';

@Component({
  selector: 'app-root',
  templateUrl: './app.component.html',
  styleUrls: ['./app.component.css'],
})
export class AppComponent implements OnInit {
  loadService = inject(LoadService);
  toaster = inject(ToastrService);
  title = 'gym-diary';

  ngOnInit(): void {
    if (environment.production) {
      this.toaster.info('Production Build!');
    } else {
      this.toaster.info('Development Build!');
    }
  }
}
```

In this change, we are using the toaster service (for more details, refer to *Chapter 8, Improving Backend Integrations: the Interceptor Pattern*) to indicate, when the user enters the page, which environment they are in.

Let's run our application using the `ng serve` command, and we will get the following result:

Figure 12.8 – Application in development mode

If we log in to our application, we can see, by looking at the developer tools in the **Networks** tab, that the application is making requests to our local backend. To run our Angular project as a production build, we can use the following command:

```
ng serve --configuration production
```

When accessing our application, we can see in the message on the screen that requests are made to the service published in our cloud service:

Figure 12.9 – Application in production mode

With our service prepared for multiple environments, we can now see how we can better prepare it for deployment in the next section.

Preparing the production bundle

The environmental needs of a frontend application running in production are different from the development environment we have seen so far in the book.

When we are developing, we look for speed in compilation, powerful debugging, and profiling tools to analyze our code, as well as generating boilerplate code, among other features.

Even though it costs more to process on our local machine, requires more space to generate instrumented bundles to be able to perform debugging, and requires greater network consumption to download development tools, all of this is important for the team's productivity, and the Angular framework delivers it in a robust ecosystem.

When we are talking about frontend web code running in production, the objective is almost the opposite. We want our code to be as small and optimized as possible, to be downloaded and executed by our users in the most performant way possible.

With this objective in mind, the Angular framework has a robust and simple build tool for generating the production package.

To run it, we need to use the following command in our `project` folder:

```
ng build
```

This command will create the package that we will run in production in the `dist` folder of our project.

But to deepen our knowledge of the Angular framework, let's understand what the basis for this build process is. The answer is in the `angular.json` file. Let's analyze some important properties of the build:

```
"configurations": {
  "production": {
    "budgets": [
      {
        "type": "initial",
        "maximumWarning": "500kb",
        "maximumError": "1mb"
      },
      {
        "type": "anyComponentStyle",
        "maximumWarning": "2kb",
        "maximumError": "4kb"
      }
    ],
    "outputHashing": "all"
  },
  . . .
  "defaultConfiguration": "production"
}
```

In the `configurations` property, we have definitions of the types of environments that we can have in our project. Initially, the Angular CLI creates two configurations: production and development.

In the production configuration, we have the `budgets` property, which determines the maximum size that our package must have in addition to defining the maximum size that a unitary component must have.

If your project exceeds this size, Angular may show a warning in the production console or even not build your project.

This is important because we need to generate the smallest file possible as this results in a greater perception of performance for our users, especially if they are using a device on a 3G network.

One way to reduce file sizes is to use Angular's lazy-loading capabilities (for more details on this feature, see *Chapter 2, Organizing Your Application*).

The `outputHashing` attribute ensures that the files generated by the application have their names added to a hash.

This is important because most public clouds and **Content Delivery Networks** (**CDNs**) cache the application based on the name of the files. When we generate a new version of our app, we want this cache to be invalidated to deliver the new version to our users.

Finally, the `defaultConfiguration` property determines that if no parameter is passed, the `ng build` command will execute with the configuration indicated in it, in this case, production.

These configurations can be expanded and new ones created depending on your project needs. In our case, we will leave it with the default configuration.

When running the build in production configurations, Angular performs the following processes:

- **Ahead-of-Time (AOT) compilation**: Angular compiles templates and CSS files in addition to TypeScript files.
- **Production mode**: The application has some validations optimized for running in production.
- **Bundling**: It bundles all component files, templates, services and libraries in files separated by modules.
- **Minification**: From the files generated by TypeScript, it concatenates and eliminates whitespace and comments to generate the smallest files possible.
- **Uglification**: It rewrites generated code for variables, function names, and small, cryptic modules to make it difficult to reverse engineer the frontend code delivered to the user's browser.
- **Dead code elimination**: Also known as **tree shaking**, this is the process of not including components in bundles that are not referenced in the code and do not need to be present in the production package.

All these processes are done with the `ng build` command and with the configuration that was set when your project was created. It is important to note that this process improves with each new version of Angular and is another reason to always keep your project up to date with the latest versions.

In the next section, we will create a Docker image with our code built and run by the Nginx web server.

Mounting a Docker image with Nginx

Until this chapter, we have been using the web server included in the Angular package to run our application locally. Although very competent, it focuses purely on the developer's experience and does not have the performance and scalability capabilities required by the production environment.

For this purpose, we use production-grade web servers. One of the most popular is Nginx (pronounced *Engine X*).

To configure it, we need to create a file in the root of our project called `nginx.default.conf` and add the following to it:

```
server {
  listen 80;
  sendfile on;
  default_type application/octet-stream;
  gzip on;
  gzip_http_version 1.1;
  gzip_disable        "MSIE [1-6]\.";
  gzip_min_length    1100;
  gzip_vary          on;
  gzip_proxied        expired no-cache no-store private auth;
  gzip_types          text/plain text/css application/json application/
javascript application/x-javascript text/xml application/xml
application/xml+rss text/javascript;
  gzip_comp_level    9;
  root /usr/share/nginx/html;
  location / {
    try_files $uri $uri/ /index.html =404;
  }
}
```

In this configuration file, the first three properties (`listen`, `sendfile`, and `default_type`) aim to configure the exposed port and prepare the server to send our project's package files.

The properties starting with `gzip` configure the delivery of files with the native web compression data `gzip`, further reducing the files delivered to our user's browser.

The last part of the file determines the first page to be served. As we are in a **Single-Page Application** (**SPA**), the first file to be delivered is `index.html`.

With this configuration, we can run Nginx, but instead of installing it natively on our local machine, we will use Docker to run it.

Docker is a tool widely used in today's modern systems and aims to compartmentalize an application's environment. In other words, by configuring a file, we can create an environment for our application where it can be run both on our local machine and on a cloud provider with the same dependencies and versions.

Let's exemplify its use by first creating a file called .dockerignore in our project's root and adding the following to it:

```
node_modules
```

Using the .gitignore file as an example, we are ensuring that the node_modules folder will not be copied to the image. Keep in mind that the image and the service that will be run from it (called a container in the Docker ecosystem) is as if it were a new machine and we will only copy what our application needs to run.

The next step is to create the dockerfile file and add the following code to it:

```
FROM node:18-alpine as build
COPY package.json package-lock.json ./
RUN npm ci && mkdir /gym-app && mv ./node_modules ./gym-app/
WORKDIR /gym-app
COPY . .
RUN npm run build
FROM nginx:1.25-alpine
COPY nginx.default.conf /etc/nginx/conf.d/default.conf
RUN rm -rf /usr/share/nginx/html/*
COPY --from=build /gym-app/dist/gym-diary /usr/share/nginx/html
CMD ["nginx", "-g", "daemon off;"]
```

In this file, we are using the multi-stage build technique to create our image. First, we build the application and then use the result of this build to create the final image. This way, our image becomes smaller and more optimized.

The first stage, which we call build here, is based on the node:18-alpine image, which is a minimal image with the Alpine Linux distribution and version 18 of Node.js included.

Then, the package.json and package-lock.json files are copied and the npm ci command is run to install the package.

Then, with the COPY . . command, all project code is copied (except the node_module folder).

At the end of this stage, our application bundle is generated using the npm run build command.

The next stage, which will be production, is based on the nginx:1.25-alpine image because to run the web server, we only need a Linux distribution such as Nginx installed.

The next task is to copy the configuration file for the Nginx installation, delete the example file that comes with the tool, and copy the files generated in the previous stage to this one.

The line `["nginx", "-g", "daemon off;"]` runs Nginx and makes it ready to deliver our application.

To mount the image, right-click on the `dockerfile` file in VSCode and select the **Build Image** option.

To run the Docker container locally, use the following command:

```
docker run -p 8080:80 gymdiary
```

By accessing the `http://localhost:8080` URL, we have our application running in production mode. Another way to put our project on the web is by using Azure Static Web Apps. We will work on this in the next section.

Deploying a page to Azure Static Web Apps

With the Docker image we created, we can run our project on any cloud provider that offers container services. However, there are other ways to deploy our Angular project.

One of these alternatives is Azure Static Web Apps, a service that specializes in web page design and allows automatic integration with GitHub. Let's see it in practice in our project.

The first requirement is that your project is on GitHub, as shown in the following screenshot:

Figure 12.10 – GitHub repository for frontend project

If you have copied the project repository, place the `gym-diary` folder in your own GitHub project.

To configure the Azure service, go to the account portal and search for `Static Web Apps`.

Click on the **Create Static Web App** button and the service form will be presented to you.

In the first part, we have the following fields:

- **Subscription**: Select your Azure subscription.

- **Resource Group**: Create or define a group for this service. In Azure, every resource must be linked to a resource group.

- **Name**: Provide a name for your frontend project.

- **Plan type**: Select the tier of your environment. The more resources, the higher the cost, but for our example, we will just use the free plan.

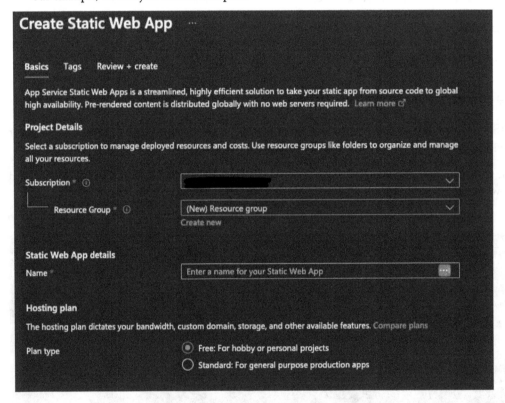

Figure 12.11 – Azure Static Web App creation

- **Source**: In this field, we identify whether our project is on GitHub or in the Azure repository.

- **Organization**: The name of the GitHub user or organization that you want to select the repository from. It is important that your user has high access permission, such as maintainer or admin.

- **Repository**: Azure will list all the repositories that you have access to in the selected organization..

- **Branch**: The branch of the repository that you want to deploy.

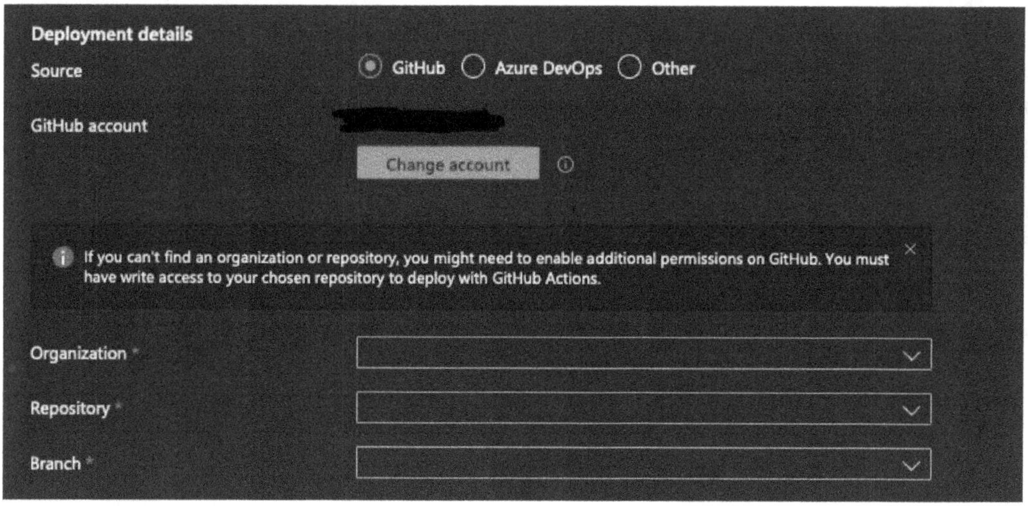

Figure 12.12 – Deployment details configuration

In the second part, we have the specific configuration for our project using Angular:

- **Build Presets**: The Azure service supports several frontend technologies. Here, in this case, we will choose **Angular**.

- **App location**: We must indicate within GitHub which folder contains the Angular project, as our project is in the root of the repo. We can leave it as /.

- **Api location**: This is an optional field if you want to point to a backend service deployed in Azure. Here, in this example, we are going to leave it blank.

- **Output location**: We must place the location where the build is generated within the repository. In the case of our project, we will set dist/gym-diary/.

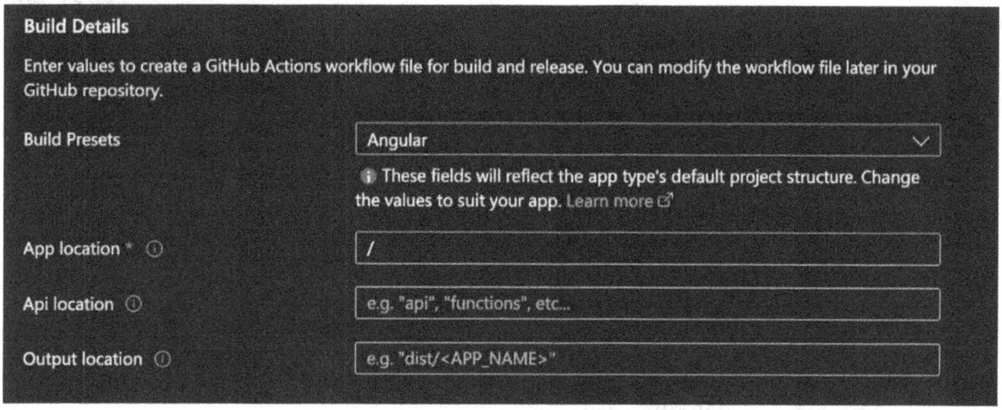

Figure 12.13 – Preset settings

Once done, click on **Review and Create**, and on the next screen, confirm the operation. Azure will begin processing, and once ready, it will display the created service dashboard:

Figure 12.14 – Service dashboard created

In the **URL** field, you will see the URL created by Azure for our project. Select it and our system will be presented as soon as the deploy status is **Ready**. So, we have our project up and running in the cloud. You can configure other settings, such as adding your own URL, although remember that some settings are not available in the free plan.

The most interesting thing about this feature is that it implements a GitHub action in our repository:

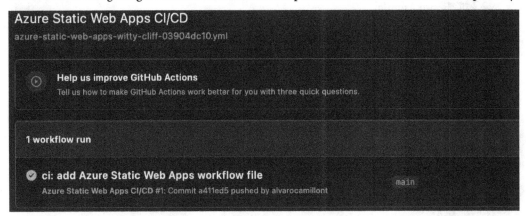

Figure 12.15 – GitHub action

What is a GitHub action? It is a GitHub feature that allows the creation and execution of scripts to automate tasks, such as, in our example, deploying to the Azure service.

With our configuration, the Azure wizard created and ran the script in our GitHub repository.

A bonus is that our generated script is configured to execute and deploy with each push we make to the repository, updating our application deployed in the cloud.

Summary

In this chapter, we explored the techniques and capabilities of Angular when deploying our application to production.

We started by uploading our backend to the cloud, where it will be available for our frontend application.

Then, we adapted our application to differentiate the development environment and the production environment using the Angular feature of `environment.ts` files.

We explored the `ng build` command and all the tasks that Angular performs for us to make our application as lean as possible to be faster for our users.

We learned about Docker and how we can package our Angular application to run on a web server such as Nginx regardless of the type of machine our application runs on.

Finally, we learned about another way to deploy to the cloud with the Azure Static Web Apps service and saw how it automates this process by creating a GitHub action script.

In the next chapter, we will explore the latest Angular innovations, including Angular Signals.

The Angular Renaissance

Our applications need to continually evolve, and to meet this need, the Angular framework and its ecosystem also continue to evolve.

In this chapter, we will learn about the latest features of Angular. While many of them are still in the developer preview phase, it is important for us to get a glimpse of what the future holds for this incredible framework.

In this chapter, we will cover the following topics:

- Updating your project with the Angular CLI
- Using a new way to create templates – control flow
- Improving the user experience using the `defer` command
- Creating transitions between pages – view transactions
- Simplifying application states – Angular Signals

By the end of this chapter, you will have learned how to stay up to date with future versions of the framework and how to update your project.

Technical requirements

To follow the instructions in this chapter, you'll need the following:

- Visual Studio Code (`https://code.visualstudio.com/Download`)
- Node.js 18 or higher (`https://nodejs.org/en/download/`)

The code files for this chapter are available at `https://github.com/PacktPublishing/Angular-Design-Patterns-and-Best-Practices/tree/main/ch13`.

During the course of this chapter, remember to run the backend of the application found in the `gym-diary-backend` folder with the `npm start` command.

Updating your project with the Angular CLI

The Angular framework is continually evolving with new features and optimizations, but to help communities and developers keep organized and their applications up to date, the Angular team uses semantic versioning to number their releases.

A semantic version number is composed of three parts and each part has the following representation:

- **Major**: A number that is increased every time there is a change in the framework, which in turn requires us to change something in our application so that it continues to work, also known as a **breaking change**

- **Minor**: A number that is increased when the new version has a new functionality that we can use, but if we don't use it, we don't need to change our application

- **Patch**: A number that is increased when there is a correction to the framework and we do not need to change our code; this is widely used for versions that have security corrections

In this book, we are working with version 16.2.0 of Angular, and the next version will be 17.0.0, which will bring new functionality and also some breaking changes. While the the term "breaking changes" is used, we should note that the Angular team has taken more and more care with these changes and currently, they only affect very specific cases that the vast majority of applications are not affected by.

In addition to rigorous versioning, the Angular team takes care to release major releases every six months, allowing the team to plan application updates. You may ask, should I always update the Angular version of my application? The answer is yes, and here are some reasons:

- Every new version brings internal improvements to the framework that improve the rendering engines, which can make your application faster and the build time and the bundle size smaller and more optimized

- New features give you more possibilities to create better experiences for your users

- It provides security updates and framework vulnerability fixes

It is important to highlight that the Angular team is committed to making corrections (long-term support) for up to two major versions before the current one, which means that using old versions of Angular can leave your application vulnerable to new security breaches. However, the task of updating the Angular version of an application is not that complex as the Angular CLI helps to automate the entire process. Let's update our project to version 17 of Angular to use the new features in this chapter.

On your operating system's command line, in the gym-diary project folder, use the following command:

```
ng update @angular/core@17 @angular/cli@17
```

With this command, the Angular CLI will update all Angular packages from the `package.json` file. Furthermore, it will analyze all your code in search of situations where it needs to be changed due to a breaking change. Also, if possible, it will update your code for you. If this is not possible, it will indicate what type of correction should be made, but again this only happens in very specific corner cases.

After the update is complete, to ensure that the application continues to work after the process, we can run unit tests and end-to-end tests. For more details about the tests, see *Chapter 10, Design for Tests: Best Practices*.

With our updated project, we can explore the new syntax for HTML templates, which we will see in the next section.

Using a new way to create templates – control flow

Since version 2 of the framework, the HTML template syntax has remained relatively stable and without much evolution. By using custom properties, we can evaluate conditions and iterate over lists and other forms of flow control to create visualization logic in components. The `*ngIf`, `*ngFor`, and `*ngSwitch` directives are used to improve the developer experience, internally generating the elements in the HTML. You can read more about this in *Chapter 4, Components and Pages*.

Starting with version 17, the Angular team introduced a new form of control flow in HTML. The syntax in this version is in developer preview, which means that it is stable for production but may have changes in future versions. Let's refactor our code to use the syntax and see the difference in practice.

In the `app.component.html` file, we will change the following:

```
@if (loadService.isLoading) {
  <app-loading-overlay />
}
<router-outlet></router-outlet>
```

Here, we can notice the first new structure of the new control flow, `if`. Using the command in the HTML template with the @ symbol, we apply the conditional statement as in TypeScript, evaluating whether the function or variable is true or false.

The novelty of the syntax is that we now have the `@else` instruction facilitating the chaining of conditionals, without the need to use the `ng-template` directive for this purpose.

We will refactor the `list-entries.component.html` file as follows:

```
<section class="mb-8">
  <h2 class="mb-4 text-xl font-bold">List of entries</h2>
  <ul class="rounded border shadow">
    @for (item of exerciseList; track item.id) {
    <li>
      <app-entry-item
```

```
            [exercise-set]="item"
            (deleteEvent)="deleteEvent.emit($event)"
            (editEvent)="editEvent.emit($event)"
        />
      </li>
      } @empty {
        <div>
          No Items!
        </div>
      }
    </ul>
  </section>
```

In this example, we are using the @for instruction to replace the *ngFor directive. We provide the name of the variable that will receive the list iteration, in this case, item, and the list itself, in this component, named exerciseList.

In *Chapter 4, Components and Pages*, we learned the good practice of using the trackBy property of the *ngFor directive to improve list rendering performance. This good practice is now mandatory in the new @for syntax, and in this case, it is even simpler as we can simply pass the attribute that Angular should check.

A new element is the @empty instruction, which indicates what should be shown if the list in question is empty.

The new @for instruction, in addition to improving the development experience, is also 90% faster, according to the Angular team, when rendering lists than the previous solution. That's because control statements aren't just sugar syntax for directives; the template engine has been redesigned and the instructions manipulate Angular's internal DOM rendering elements.

Finally, let's refactor the new-entry-form-reactive.component.html file as follows:

```
. . .
@if (entryForm.get('date')?.invalid && entryForm.get('date')?.touched)
{
    <div class="mt-1 text-red-500">Date is required.</div>
    }
. . .
@if (showSuggestions) {
    <ul
      class="absolute z-10 mt-2 w-auto rounded border border-gray-300
bg-white"
      >
        @for (suggestion of exercises$ | async; track suggestion.id) {
```

```
      <li
        class="cursor-pointer px-3 py-2 hover:bg-blue-500 hover:text-
  white"
        (click)="selectExercise(suggestion.description)"
      >
        {{ suggestion.description }}
      </li>
      }
    </ul>
    } @if (entryForm.get('exercise')?.invalid &&
    entryForm.get('exercise')?.touched) {
    <div class="mt-1 text-red-500">Exercise is required.</div>
    }
. . .
@if (entryForm.get('reps')?.invalid && entryForm.get('reps')?.touched)
{
    <div class="mt-1 text-red-500">
      Reps is required and must be a positive number.
    </div>
    }@else if ( entryForm.get('reps')?.errors?.['isNotMultiple'] &&
    entryForm.get('reps')?.touched) {
    <div class="mt-1 text-red-500">
      Reps is required and must be multiple of 3.
    </div>
    }
```

In this file, we are replacing the conditionals that evaluate form errors with the @if statement. For the @for instruction that we use to render the list of exercises, we can notice that the use of the async pipe remains very similar to the *ngFor directive, and we added track to further improve the rendering of the list. Finally, we are using the @else if command to chain two conditionals.

We can note that we do not need to perform any additional configuration to use the flow control syntax because this functionality is fully compatible with the previous mechanics and they can coexist in the same project and even in the same file.

The Angular team even created a migration command in the Angular CLI, as follows:

```
ng g @angular/core:control-flow
```

In the next section, we will see a new possibility that this template refactoring provides to our application, the option of lazy loading components in our HTML templates.

Improving the user experience using the defer command

The main intention behind the new HTML template flow control syntax was to have a new basis for building new possibilities in the framework's templates. The first new feature made possible by the syntax is the `defer` instruction, with which it is possible to lazy load components directly from the HTML template.

We learned in *Chapter 2, Organizing Your Application*, that the best practice is to separate your application into functionality modules and configure Angular to load these modules in a lazy way. This means that the module and its components would only be loaded if the user accessed a certain route, resulting in smaller bundles and better performance of your application, especially if your user does not have a good internet connection (such as 3G).

The `defer` command has the same purpose but instead of working for modules, it works for `standalone` components. We studied `standalone` components in *Chapter 11, Micro Frontend with Angular Elements*.

We will start our refactoring by transforming the exercise list components into a `standalone` component. In the `diary.component.ts` file, make the following changes:

```
@Component({
    standalone: true,
    templateUrl: './diary.component.html',
    styleUrls: ['./diary.component.css'],
    imports: [ListEntriesComponent, NewItemButtonComponent],
})
```

In the preceding code, we have included the `standalone` attribute set to `true` and added the components it depends on directly using the `imports` attribute.

We will do the same procedure in the `EntryItemComponent` component:

```
@Component({
    selector: 'app-entry-item',
    standalone: true,
    templateUrl: './entry-item.component.html',
    styleUrls: ['./entry-item.component.css'],
    imports: [DatePipe],
})
```

In this component, in addition to the `standalone` property, we need to add the dependency so that the date pipe works. It is necessary to note that the standalone component needs to have its dependencies declaratively in the `imports` attribute, since it is not linked to any Angular module.

To lazy load the template, we will also convert the `NewItemButtonComponent` component into a standalone one:

```
@Component({
  selector: 'app-new-item-button',
  templateUrl: './new-item-button.component.html',
  styleUrls: ['./new-item-button.component.css'],
  standalone: true,
})
```

The last component to be converted into a standalone component is `ListEntriesComponent`, changing it as follows:

```
@Component({
  selector: 'app-list-entries',
  standalone: true,
  templateUrl: './list-entries.component.html',
  styleUrls: ['./list-entries.component.css'],
  imports: [EntryItemComponent],
})
```

In this example, we added the `EntryItemComponent` dependency to the `import` attribute.

> **Important note**
>
> The unit tests were also adjusted to consider the component dependencies in the `TestBed` definition, and you can find the test code in the GitHub repository of this chapter.

The last adjustment must be made in the `DiaryModule` module:

```
@NgModule({
  declarations: [
    NewEntryFormTemplateComponent,
    NewEntryFormReactiveComponent,
  ],
  imports: [
    CommonModule,
    DiaryRoutingModule,
    RouterModule,
    FormsModule,
    ReactiveFormsModule,
  ],
})
export class DiaryModule {}
```

As we will dynamically load the components that were converted to standalone, we have to remove these components from the `declarations` attribute of the module.

After this preparation, we can use the `defer` command in the `diary.component.html` file:

```
@defer {
  <app-list-entries
    [exerciseList]="exerciseList"
    (deleteEvent)="deleteItem($event)"
    (editEvent)="editEntry($event)"
  />
}
```

To use the `defer` command, we must create a block that includes the components that we want to lazy load.

If we run our application and analyze the **Networks** tab, we will notice that specific bundles are loaded when the screen is rendered:

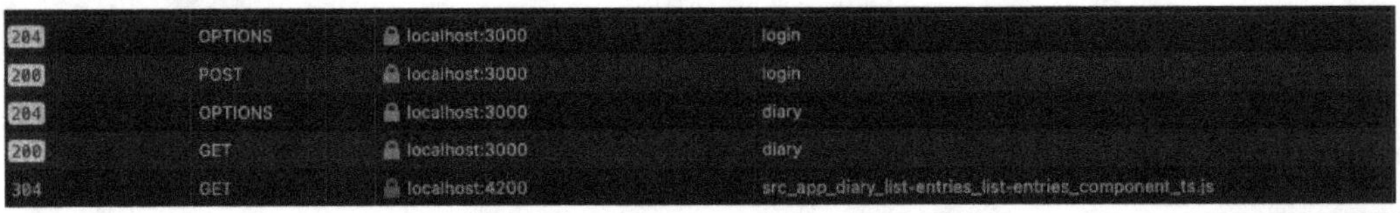

Figure 12.1 – Lazy-loaded bundle

We can see that the effect is similar to the lazy loading of a route module, but `defer` has other interesting options. Let's see this in practice by changing our code:

```
. . .
@defer (on hover(trigger)){
  <app-list-entries
    [exerciseList]="exerciseList"
    (deleteEvent)="deleteItem($event)"
    (editEvent)="editEntry($event)"
  />
}
. . .
  <button
    #trigger
    class="rounded bg-blue-500 px-4 py-2 font-bold text-white
hover:bg-blue-700"
    (click)="newList()"
  >
    Server Sync
  </button>
. . .
```

With the `on hover(trigger)` condition, the list is loaded when we hover over the **Server Sync** button. This is just an example; the `defer` command opens up a range of opportunities for fine-tuning the user experience. The `defer` command has the following conditions:

- `on immediate`: The component will be loaded the moment the screen is rendered.

- `on idle`: The component will be loaded on the first call to the browser `requestIdleCallback` API. This API allows non-blocking processing in the browser and is the default behavior of the `defer` command.

- `on hover(target)`: We can define another interface component and loading will occur when the user hovers over this component.

- `on timer(time)`: Allows us to define in milliseconds when the component will be loaded after the interface is rendered.

- `on viewport(target)`: When the target component is in the browser's viewport, the child components will be loaded. This behavior is ideal for loading a component that is located after the user has scrolled to the end of the page.

- `on interaction(target)`: It has a similar behavior to *on hover*, but it will be triggered by some interaction, such as a click.

- `when (condition)`: Allows us to control the loading of the component imperatively, through a Boolean attribute, or a function that returns a Boolean.

Complementing the `defer` command, we have other commands that we can use. Returning to our code, we will change it as follows:

```
@defer {
  <app-list-entries
    [exerciseList]="exerciseList"
    (deleteEvent)="deleteItem($event)"
    (editEvent)="editEntry($event)"
  />
} @loading {
<div>Loading</div>
} @placeholder {
<div>PlaceHolder</div>
} @error {
<div>Error</div>
}
```

These complementary commands have the following functions:

- `@loading`: Presents the content of the block while the components of the `defer` block are loaded

- `@placeholder`: Displays the content of the block, while the components of the `defer` block do not start loading, for example, if the user does not hover over the given target

- `@error`: Displays the content of the block if an error occurs when loading the components of the `defer` block

There are many possibilities that we have with this `defer` command in our templates, and we should explore them to improve our users' experience. But note that we should not lazy load all the components of a screen. We need to use the `defer` command on large components or components that are not essential for the page we are building.

In the next section, we will explore how to improve the experience of transitions between routes in our application.

Creating transitions between pages – view transactions

As frontend developers, we need to worry about the technical performance of our applications. Small UI details, such as the loading screen that we created in *Chapter 8, Improving Backend Integrations: the Interceptor Pattern*, improve our users' perception of the application's performance. One of these UI details is the transition between pages of our application. Instead of dry loading from one route to another, we can create an animation that smooths this transition, making the user experience more pleasant.

Until version 17 of Angular, it was possible to make this animation using the standard Angular Animation package that we used earlier in the book, in the toaster animation created in *Chapter 8, Improving Backend Integrations: the Interceptor Pattern*. The way to create this animation is specific to Angular and is not very simple for designers specializing in CSS.

As of version 17 of Angular, there is support for the **View Transitions API**, a specific web API for this use case that allows you to create transition animations using pure CSS. To use it in our project, we will change the `app-routing.module.ts` file:

```
@NgModule({
  imports: [
    RouterModule.forRoot(routes, {
      bindToComponentInputs: true,
      enableViewTransitions: true,
    }),
  ],
  exports: [RouterModule],
})
export class AppRoutingModule {}
```

We are configuring Angular so that the route mechanisms will use view transitions written in CSS with the `enableViewTransitions` property. With just this change, we can notice in our application that the transition between pages has a pleasant fade-in and fade-out animation. This default animation was created by the Angular team to make developers' lives easier. But we can also customize this animation with a little CSS. In the `styles.css` file, we will create the following classes:

```
@keyframes slide-right {
  from {
    transform: translateX(40px);
  }
}
@keyframes slide-left {
  to {
    transform: translateX(-40px);
  }
}

@keyframes fade-in {
  from {
    opacity: 0;
  }
}
@keyframes fade-out {
  to {
    opacity: 0;
  }
}
```

For CSS animations, we need to define an initial and final state that we want the element to be in, in this case, the entire screen. For our example, we define a state where the screen goes to the right in the `slide-right` keyframe and goes to the left in the `slide-left` keyframe. Finally, we define the keyframes for the fade-in and fade-out effects.

Note that when we define the transition animation, we completely replace Angular's default transition animation, so we are defining the fade-in and fade-out keyframes here.

To set up the animation, let's add the following to the `styles.css` file:

```
::view-transition-old(root) {
  animation: 100ms cubic-bezier(0.4, 0, 1, 1) both fade-out,
  400ms cubic-bezier(0.4, 0, 0.2, 1) both slide-left;
}
::view-transition-new(root) {
  animation: 250ms cubic-bezier(0, 0, 0.2, 1) 90ms both fade-in,
  400ms cubic-bezier(0.4, 0, 0.2, 1) both slide-right;
}
```

The View Transitions API creates pseudo-elements in the CSS where we define the exit animation of the old page (`::view-transition-old`) and the entrance animation of the new page (`::view-transition-old`). In this case, we define that the old screen will fade out and move to the left and the new page will fade in and slide in from the right.

> **Important note**
>
> The View Transitions API was created in 2023 and is being gradually adopted by browsers. Go to `https://caniuse.com/` and check whether the browsers your users will use have support for this API.

In the next section, we will explore Angular Signals and how we can use it to simplify state control in our application.

Simplifying application states – Angular Signals

Controlling the state of a frontend application is one of the biggest challenges for a developer, as by nature, the interface is dynamic and needs to react to various user actions. Angular, with its *stacks included* philosophy, already had tools suitable for this task, and we studied in *Chapters 5, Angular Services and the Singleton Pattern*, and *Chapter 9, Exploring Reactivity with RxJS*, how to use these tools. However, despite being effective, the Angular community and team recognize that they are a bit complex for new developers and for simple cases of reactivity in frontend projects. To fill this gap, the Angular team introduced, from version 17 onward, a new element to the framework, called Signals.

According to the Angular documentation, a signal is a wrapper around a value that notifies consumers when that value changes. An analogy that you can associate with a signal is a cell in a spreadsheet. It can contain a value and we can create formulas in other cells that use its value to create other values.

Before refactoring our application, let's illustrate this with a simpler example:

```
let a = signal<number>(2);
let b = signal<number>(3);
let sum = computed(() => a() + b());
console.log(sum());
```

To create a signal, we use the `signal` function, where we define what type of value it will store and declare an initial value for it. A signal can be writable or read-only; in this case, the variables a and b are writable. The variable c is also a signal but of a specific type, called computed. The computed type is, in our analogy of a spreadsheet, a cell that contains a formula where you can read the values of other cells to determine its value. Finally, we are reading the value of the signal by simply calling it as a function. The result of this code snippet is the value 5.

We will now change the example:

```
let a = signal<number>(2);
let b = signal<number>(3);
let sum = computed((() => a() + b());
console.log(sum());
a.set(9);
console.log(sum());
```

In this change, we are updating the value of signal a using the set method. When reading the sum signal, we can notice that the value was updated to 12. Notice that the calculation reacts in real time just like it would in a spreadsheet..

Another way to update the value of a writable signal is by using the update method:

```
let a = signal<number>(2);
let b = signal<number>(3);
let sum = computed((() => a() + b());
console.log(sum());
a.set(9);
console.log(sum());
b.update((oldValue) => oldValue * 2);
console.log(sum());
```

The update method allows you to update the signal based on the last value contained there.

Despite being simple, signal allows many possibilities as it can contain any type of value, from primitive ones such as numeric, string, and Boolean to complex objects.

We will refactor our project to use signals, starting with the LoadService service:

```
export class LoadService {
  isLoading = signal<Boolean>(false);
  showLoader() {
    this.isLoading.set(true);
  }
  hideLoader() {
    this.isLoading.set(false);
  }
}
```

Here, we are exchanging the isLoading attribute for the isLoading signal, simplifying the service. We will change the AppComponent component template as follows:

```
@if (loadService.isLoading()) {
  <app-loading-overlay />
```

```
}
<router-outlet></router-outlet>
```

To read the contents of the signal, we call it as if it were a function. Normally, it is not a good practice to call a function in a template, due to unnecessary processing. However, the signal was created and optimized to be read in the template, so in this case, there is no problem.

The next task will be to refactor the list of journal entries so that we no longer manage the list but leave everything to the `ExerciseSetsService` service. We'll start by changing the `ExerciseSetsService` service as follows:

```
export class ExerciseSetsService {
  . . .
  exerciseList = signal<ExerciseSetList>([] as ExerciseSetList);
  getInitialList() {
    const headers = new HttpHeaders().set('X-TELEMETRY', 'true');
    this.httpClient
      .get<ExerciseSetListAPI>(this.url, { headers })
      .pipe(map((api) => api?.items))
      .subscribe((list) => this.exerciseList.set(list));
  }
  deleteItem(id: string) {
    this.httpClient.delete<boolean>(`${this.url}/${id}`).subscribe(()
=> {
    this.exerciseList.update((list) =>
      list.filter((exerciseSet) => exerciseSet.id !== id)
    );
    });
  }
  . . .
}
```

In the preceding code block, we created the `exerciseList` signal by declaring it to contain `ExerciseSetList` and initializing it with an empty list. Then, we changed the `getInitialList` method toupdate the `exerciseList` signal based on the API return. We also changed the `delete` method to update the signal after deleting the diary entry.

As we are changing the behavior of the function, we also need to exclude the `diaryResolver` function as now, the service will manage the query in the API and the component will consume the created signal.

In the `ListEntriesComponent` component, we will refactor to consume the signal list we created:

```
export class ListEntriesComponent {
  @Output() editEvent = new EventEmitter<ExerciseSet>();
```

```
@Output() deleteEvent = new EventEmitter<string>();

private exerciseSetsService = inject(ExerciseSetsService);
exerciseList = this.exerciseSetsService.exerciseList;
}
```

In the preceding code block, we replace the component's input with the ExerciseSetsService service and receive the exerciseList signal from it.

We will change the ListEntriesComponent component template as follows:

```
<section class="mb-8">
  <h2 class="mb-4 text-xl font-bold">List of entries</h2>
  <ul class="rounded border shadow">
  @for (item of exerciseList(); track item.id) {
    <li>
      <app-entry-item
        [exercise-set]="item"
        (deleteEvent)="deleteEvent.emit($event)"
        (editEvent)="editEvent.emit($event)"
      />
    </li>
    } @empty {
      <div>
        No Items!
      </div>
    }
  </ul>
</section>
```

The @for command is prepared to read the content of a signal, including checking the type of value contained in it.

To finish this refactoring, we will change the template of the 'DiaryComponent' component:

```
<app-list-entries
  (deleteEvent)="deleteItem($event)"
  (editEvent)="editEntry($event)"
/>
```

We removed the exercise list from the app-list-entries component as it will manage the state itself.

After changing the template, we can change the `DiaryComponent` component:

```
ngOnInit(): void {
  this.exerciseSetsService.getInitialList();
}
deleteItem(id: string) {
  this.exerciseSetsService.deleteItem(id);
}
```

As the state is now managed by the `ExerciseSetsService` service, we are simplifying the component by just calling the service's methods, without having to manage subscriptions to observables.

With the state managed by Signals, we can add a new feature here on this screen. Let's assume that we need to inform the total training volume in the diary, that is, the total amount of exercise performed.

To have this information and react to events such as the deletion or inclusion of an entry, we can use Angular Signals!

In the `DiaryComponent` component, we will make the following change:

```
volume = computed<number>(() =>
  this.exerciseSetsService
    .exerciseList()
    .reduce(
      (volume, exerciseSet) => volume + exerciseSet.reps *
exerciseSet.sets,
      0
    )
);
```

We create a new computed signal called `'volume'` and perform the calculation in it based on the value contained in the `'exerciseList'` signal.

To use this new signal, let's change the template:

```
<header class="bg-blue-500 py-4 text-white">
  <div class="mx-auto max-w-6xl px-4">
    <h1 class="text-2xl font-bold">Workout diary - Total Volume:
{{volume()}} </h1>
  </div>
</header>
```

We are consuming the `volume` signal by calling the signal directly in the template. By running our project, we can notice that this `volume` signal reacts to the changes we make in our list of exercises.

Figure 12.2 – Lazy-loaded bundle

Signals are elements that will be increasingly improved by the Angular team, giving more control over the reactivity of our applications. An important point that we need to pay attention to is that Signals will not replace RxJS; in fact, they complement each other as we still need observables to control asynchronous flows and more complex flows, as we studied in *Chapter 9, Exploring Reactivity with RxJS*.

Summary

In this chapter, we explored the possibilities that the future of the Angular framework can offer us. We learned how to update our project to new versions of Angular, an ongoing activity as the framework continues to evolve. We understood how Angular versioning works and the importance of continually updating our project, from the point of view of security, performance, and new features. Then, we changed our application to use the new template expressions, which, in addition to simplifying, can, depending on the case, improve the performance of our applications. With this improvement in template expressions, we looked at the `defer` expression, which allows for the lazy loading of components within templates, giving us new options for optimizing interfaces with complex components. We also learned how to use the View Transactions API to improve our users' experience with animations between page changes. Finally, we explored Angular Signals and simplified the state management of our application with this new element that complements RxJs. Angular is a framework that never stops evolving, as our users never stop demanding new features. In this chapter, we learned how to stay up to date with Angular.

Index

A

B

C

child component
communication from 68-70
classes 40-46
component modules 28
components 55
communication between 60-62
creating 56-59
properties 58
component testing 177, 178
Container component 65
Content Delivery Networks (CDNs) 212
control flow 223
custom validations 104-107
Cypress 167
for end-to-end (E2E) tests 179-184

D

data consumption
optimizing 157, 158
data handling
operators transformation 151, 152
data validation 101-103
dead code elimination 212
defer command
used, for improving user experience 226-230
dependency injection pattern 78, 79
development environment
configuring 7
Docker image
mounting, with Nginx 213-215
Dumb component 65
dynamic routes 116

E

ECMAScript modules (ESM) 25
EditorConfig 8
URL 8
encapsulation of attributes 41
end-to-end tests (E2E tests) 166, 167
with Cypress 179-184
environments
differentiating 207-210
ESLint 8
URL 8
events
propagating, from nested components 70-73
exploratory tests 167

F

filter operators 157, 158
Fira Code font 9
URL 10
frontend business rules
examples 76
functions
creating 47, 48

G

GCP
URL 202
Git Extension Pack 7
URL 7
GitHub action 218
Gym Diary application 112
dynamic routes 116-122
error page and title, defining 113-116
experience, optimizing 129-131

www.packtpub.com

Subscribe to our online digital library for full access to over 7,000 books and videos, as well as industry leading tools to help you plan your personal development and advance your career. For more information, please visit our website.

Why subscribe?

- Spend less time learning and more time coding with practical eBooks and Videos from over 4,000 industry professionals

- Improve your learning with Skill Plans built especially for you

- Get a free eBook or video every month

- Fully searchable for easy access to vital information

- Copy and paste, print, and bookmark content

Did you know that Packt offers eBook versions of every book published, with PDF and ePub files available? You can upgrade to the eBook version at packtpub.com and as a print book customer, you are entitled to a discount on the eBook copy. Get in touch with us at customercare@packtpub.com for more details.

At www.packtpub.com, you can also read a collection of free technical articles, sign up for a range of free newsletters, and receive exclusive discounts and offers on Packt books and eBooks.

Other Books You May Enjoy

If you enjoyed this book, you may be interested in these other books by Packt:

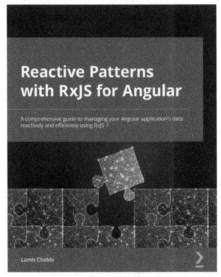

Reactive Patterns with RxJS for Angular

Lamis Chebbi

ISBN: 978-1-80181-151-4

- Understand how to use the marble diagram and read it for designing reactive applications
- Work with the latest features of RxJS 7
- Build a complete Angular app reactively, from requirement gathering to deploying it
- Become well-versed with the concepts of streams, including transforming, combining, and composing them
- Explore the different testing strategies for RxJS apps, their advantages, and drawbacks
- Understand memory leak problems in web apps and techniques to avoid them
- Discover multicasting in RxJS and how it can resolve complex problems

Learning Angular, Fourth Edition

Aristeidis Bampakos, Pablo Deeleman

ISBN: 978-1-80324-060-2

- Use the Angular CLI to scaffold, build, and deploy a new Angular application
- Build components, the basic building blocks of an Angular application
- Discover new Angular Material components such as Google Maps, YouTube, and multi-select dropdowns
- Understand the different types of templates supported by Angular
- Create HTTP data services to access APIs and provide data to components
- Learn how to build Angular apps without modules in Angular 15.x with standalone APIs
- Improve your debugging and error handling skills during runtime and development

Packt is searching for authors like you

If you're interested in becoming an author for Packt, please visit `authors.packtpub.com` and apply today. We have worked with thousands of developers and tech professionals, just like you, to help them share their insight with the global tech community. You can make a general application, apply for a specific hot topic that we are recruiting an author for, or submit your own idea.

Hi!

I am Alvaro Camillo Neto, author of *Angular Design Patterns and Best Practices*. I really hope you enjoyed reading this book and found it useful for increasing your productivity and applications using Angular.

It would really help me (and other potential readers!) if you could leave a review on Amazon sharing your thoughts on this book.

Go to the link below or scan the QR code to leave your review:

`https://packt.link/r/1837631972`

Your review will help us to understand what's worked well in this book, and what could be improved upon for future editions, so it really is appreciated.

Best Wishes,

Alvaro Camillo Neto

Download a free PDF copy of this book

Thanks for purchasing this book!

Do you like to read on the go but are unable to carry your print books everywhere?

Is your eBook purchase not compatible with the device of your choice?

Don't worry, now with every Packt book you get a DRM-free PDF version of that book at no cost.

Read anywhere, any place, on any device. Search, copy, and paste code from your favorite technical books directly into your application.

The perks don't stop there, you can get exclusive access to discounts, newsletters, and great free content in your inbox daily

Follow these simple steps to get the benefits:

1. Scan the QR code or visit the link below

https://packt.link/free-ebook/9781837631971

2. Submit your proof of purchase
3. That's it! We'll send your free PDF and other benefits to your email directly

www.ingramcontent.com/pod-product-compliance
Lightning Source LLC
Chambersburg PA
CBHW080633060326
40690CB00021B/4919